D0455202

Concrete
Economics

STEPHEN S. COHEN
J. BRADFORD DeLONG

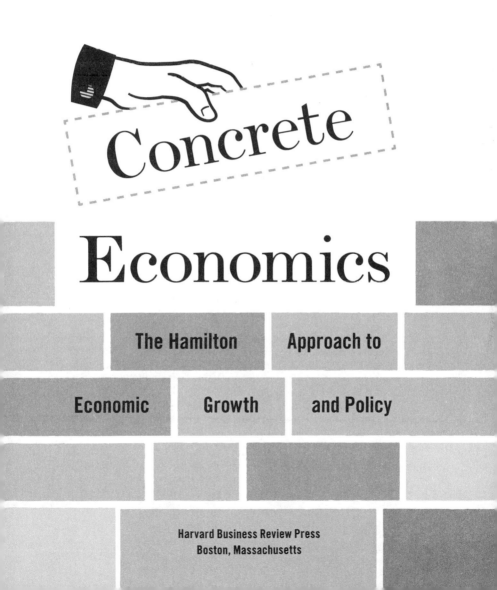

Concrete

Economics

The Hamilton Approach to

Economic Growth and Policy

Harvard Business Review Press
Boston, Massachusetts

Library of Congress Cataloging-in-Publication Data

Names: Cohen, Stephen S., author. I De Long, J. Bradford, author.
Title: Concrete economics : the Hamilton approach to economic growth and policy / Stephen S. Cohen, J. Bradford DeLong.
Description: Boston : Harvard Business Review Press, 2016.
Identifiers: LCCN 2015043604 (print) I LCCN 2015049475 (ebook) I ISBN 9781422189818 (hardback) I ISBN 9781422189825 ()
Subjects: LCSH: United States—Economic policy. I Economic development—United States—History. I history—United States—History. I BISAC: BUSINESS & ECONOMICS / Government & Business. I BUSINESS & ECONOMICS / Economics / General. I BUSINESS & ECONOMICS / Economic History.
Classification: LCC HC106.84 .C64 2016 (print) I LCC HC106.84 (ebook) I DDC 330.973—dc23
LC record available at http://lccn.loc.gov/2015043604

For Julia and Eleanor
and
For Ann Marie, Michael, and Gianna

Contents

Preface

This book does not provide any important new facts. It sets out no new economic theories. It offers no analyses of new data sets. It uses no new statistical tools. If, accidentally, we do any of these, we have in some sense failed. And we will definitely have failed if this book is not accessible, readable, and enjoyable.

Everything this book presents is—or at least was—well and widely known.

Recently, however, much seems to have been forgotten. So this book tries to do something important. It tries to remind us, in simple, concrete terms, of how the American economy, again and again, was reshaped and reinvigorated by a loveless interplay of government making broad economic policy and entrepreneurs seeking business opportunities.

This book, therefore, is about government and entrepreneurship. But it will not rehash the sturdy and well-known arguments that, to thrive, an entrepreneurial economy needs an environment characterized by a broad range of freedoms, protections, and incentives. Consider that argument axiomatic.

We are here to talk about the other important interplay of government and entrepreneurship. And it is very important.

Repeatedly, government in the United States opened a new economic space, doing what was needed to enable and encourage entrepreneurs to rush into that space, innovate, expand it and, over time, reshape the economy. Each time, and there were many, this was done pragmatically. The choice of economic space seemed obvious, and the means—while powerful interests usually had a leg up—was never the bright idea of some smart economist or distinguished committee; it was never guided by ideology, whether pure or in the guise of theory. And each time in America's long economic history— except for the most recent one, which was based on ideology rather than pragmatism—the results have been very positive indeed.

From a global, bird's-eye view, three centuries ago the world's high civilizations were roughly equal in prosperity. Today the North Atlantic nations (including a few "honorary" North Atlantic countries like Japan and Australia) are richer by a factor of at least five. And the overwhelming bulk of that divergence is due to economic policy. The post–World War II reinvigoration of Western Europe, the post-1975 rise of China, and the post-1913 relative economic decline of Argentina were, no serious thinkers dispute, predominantly driven by good and bad economic policy.

That policy matters most is clear from this global record. In successful economies, economic policy has focused on what works for people who are trying to increase productivity on the ground, not on the voices heard by madmen in authority or the doctrines of academic scribblers. That is the lesson we draw from our reading of economic history. Getting economic policy right—and getting the political economy right, so that the country can get its economic policy right—is and has been of overwhelming importance in generating prosperity. But a global, bird's-eye view cannot provide us with enough detail to understand how, exactly, or what "getting the economic policy right" really means.

For that, we have to focus.

And so this book will focus on the United States, which is, fortunately for us, the place where economic policy has been, without a doubt, the most successful over the past couple of centuries.

When we look at the United States, we find not one design of economic policy, but rather sequential redesigns as the economic environment and the policies that offer the best chance of successful medium-term growth shift.

Beginning with Alexander Hamilton, the architect of the first and most important redesign, and moving on to Abraham Lincoln and the Republican ascendancy, to Teddy Roosevelt, Franklin Roosevelt, and Dwight Eisenhower, the US government is always there, taking the lead, opening new economic spaces. It is doing so consciously. And it is doing so pragmatically—not ideologically. And it is doing so very successfully, at least until recently.

We have forgotten our history. This book seeks to remind us of our history.

Concrete
Economics

Introduction

In successful economies, economic policy has been pragmatic, not ideological. It has been concrete, not abstract.

And so it has been in the United States. From its very beginning, the United States again and again enacted policies to shift its economy onto a new growth direction—toward a new economic space of opportunity. These redirections have been big. And they have been collective choices. They have not been the emergent outcomes of innumerable individual choices aimed at achieving other goals. They have not been the unguided results of mindless evolution. They have been intelligent designs.

And they have been implemented by government, backed and pushed by powerful and often broad-based political forces, held together by a common vision of how the economy ought to change. They have then been brought to life, expanded, and transformed in extraordinary ways by entrepreneurial activity and energy. The new direction has always been selected pragmatically, not ideologically, and presented concretely. You could see it in advance—as in, "This is the kind of thing we are going to get."

Until the latest redesign, beginning in the 1980s.

Yes, there was an "invisible hand," and enormous entrepreneurial innovation and energy. But the invisible hand was repeatedly lifted at the elbow by government, and re-placed in a new position from where it could go on to perform its magic. Government signaled the direction, cleared the way, set up the path, and—when needed—provided the means. And then the entrepreneurs rushed in, innovated, took risks, profited, and expanded that new direction in ways that had not and could not have been foreseen. The new or newly transformed sectors grew, often quickly. In growing they pulled other new activities into existence around them. The effect was to reinvigorate, redirect, and reshape the economy.

This is how things have been, not just in the United States but worldwide, since even before the National Economic Council staff of Croesus, King of Lydia, came up with the game-changing idea of *coinage*. What governments have done and failed to do has been of decisive importance—even in America. Underneath the rhetoric and perpetual conflict, there is a critical though often unspoken interdependence of entrepreneurship and government—a coming-together that reshapes and grows the economy. It is a bit like tigers mating: They don't stay together and cuddle very long. But it is how America has managed to have such a successful entrepreneurial-driven economy.

The choice of new direction was based on a general perception of where America's economy ought to be going and what would be needed to move the economy in that direction. There was, always, an unsightly tangle of interests and compromises. But eyes stayed on concrete reality. Higher ideological truths or abstract theories did not direct. They were not seen as providing ready-made answers. Nor did they even frame issues. Intellectual concern and practical politics focused on how to get the new growth going—and, of course, on paying off the best-positioned interests. Changing the shape of the economy to renew and grow it was the object. The object was not to instantiate the unchanging, a priori, providential truths of any left or right political economy doctrines.

It was all very concrete, very pragmatic, very American.

Beginning in the 1980s, and continuing across a generation, the United States once again redesigned its economy. But this last time its choice of policy was not at all concrete. And it was not at all smart. For it was done very differently.

For starters, the US government was not the only government targeting the shape of the US economy. On one side, the policies of East Asian governments—first Japan, then South Korea, and then, with quickly accelerating force and scale, China—pushed their economies onto a manufacturing-export development path. On the other, the United States accommodated their export-manufacturing push by pulling resources out of import-competing sectors and implementing a set of targeted policies to shift them elsewhere, into a new growth direction, toward what were supposed to be the higher-value industries of the future. It was ideology that told us these industries were out there. It was newly minted abstract theories that told us that they were the higher-value industries of the future. But no concrete sketch of what that future shape for the economy would be was forthcoming. The invisible hand of economic magic was to pick up and realize what the stealth hand of politics had set in motion.

The two teams, Asian and American, performed a kind of cosmetic surgery on the US economy—a body-sculpting. The American accommodation of the Asian export-manufacturing push—steel, shipbuilding, automobiles, machine tools, electronics—was sold as a liposuction, fat removal. It cut away a lot of muscle. Indeed, the weight of manufacturing in the economy dropped by 9 percent: from 21.2 percent of GDP in 1979 to 12.0 percent at the peak of the last business cycle in 2007.[1] That's a big number—almost two full Pentagons: call it a Nonagon.

The Washington team performed the implant: deregulating both high and low finance; fueling real estate transaction processing; multiplying the share of economic activity devoted simply to the processing of health-insurance claims; and so forth. These sectors that were supposed to be the high-productivity, leading sectors of the economy increased by 5 percent of GDP—one full Pentagon. Today they account for a full one-fifth of the entire economy.[2] This is pure economic bloat. Impure flab. Much of it, when all goes well, is close to a zero-sum activity: no net gain.

The decline in American production of manufactured goods was not completely or primarily due, as some like to think, to a shift to a post-industrial society. That shift accounted for at most a third of the relative decline in manufacturing. We can see this by simply noting that the relative consumption of manufactured goods in no way declined proportionally to production. We still wanted the manufactures. And so we imported them. And these imports of manufactures constitute the lion's share of America's trade deficit—5 percent of GDP before the Great Recession cut imports as well as almost everything else.

To finance the purchase of all the manufactured goods we were no longer making, we did not produce other goods we could export. Instead, we accumulated debt—mountains of it. The East Asian economies were eager to build up their manufacturing capacity and capability, and our ideologically motivated redesign of the American economy told us that we didn't really care, because we didn't really want those sectors. The Asian governments were eager to extend credit and hold growing piles of dollars that were likely to depreciate. In exchange, they got the immense treasure of industries and their associated engineering communities of technological practice.

We're still living with the consequences of this last, damaging redesign.

And so America needs another redesign—and it needs it right now.

The purpose of this book is to suggest that our history has a lot to teach us about how to think about undertaking this next, necessary redesign. It is important to understand how the US government has repeatedly and intelligently redesigned the economy in the past, because the market does not undergo an intelligent redesign by itself.

In this, government once again will have to lead. It does not matter whether the US government thinks it should not lead, or whether it can't. Government—somewhere—will in any case lead the reshaping of the American economy. It might be best if that government were the American government.

Who is going to draw the new design—or even select the new design principles? A few guys who think they are smart, like us? A beltway think tank? A blue-ribbon commission? Of course not—that's not how we did it in the past. An effort at redesign is never the result of a single bright idea, with a quantitative plan for how it will ramify through the economy. No one can ever know the complex configuration that a redesign effort will eventually yield, let alone its extent. But determining the broad direction, and some enabling measures, is another, much easier undertaking.

A Little History

The history of America's imperfect but largely successful redesigns is simple and clear. Yet we have managed, over the past generation, to forget much of it and to remove it from economics courses and public debates. It is worth reviewing, for the United States should soon have another debate over whether government should take a lead in reshaping the economy or just stand back and let it evolve. Proponents of unguided evolution will claim as strongly as they can that what is good in America's economy has always just evolved via purely unguided, molecular movements, and only what is bad has been designed by the government. They will forget, for starters, Alexander Hamilton. They will forget President Eisenhower too, not to mention both Roosevelts, and presidents Lincoln and Reagan. Like or regret the outcome, that is how it happened: through deliberate efforts to reshape, selected by discussions of outcomes, not just processes. There are things that matter immensely for an economy that only government can do. If it hesitates, refuses, or botches the job, the problem does not just go away and the economy does not advance as it should.

Alexander Hamilton

Alexander Hamilton set out to redesign the agrarian economy that Britain's mercantilist policies had imposed on the North American colonies and for which America's unlimited land and limited population density so well suited it. The colonies provided tobacco and grains from their farms, furs and wood from their forests, and cotton from their plantations, and Britain provided higher-value-added manufactured goods and services such as banking and shipping. The founding fathers set out to substitute their own vision of how the American economy should develop and, in the language of modern economics, deliberately change over time the structure of America's comparative advantage. They set out to reshape the economy.

Hamilton, the founding father of the American economy, led the way, intellectually and politically, pushing policies to promote industry, commerce, and banking. Central to his view on how to redesign the American economy was the necessity of protecting America's infant industries from more competitive English producers. The playing field had to be tilted. So up went the tariff: about 25 percent in 1816. Given the huge costs of early nineteenth-century shipping, this was a formidable exercise in protectionism, as well as a major source of federal government revenues. And up it stayed—over the opposition of a nation of agriculturalists who were buyers, not producers, of manufactured goods—and to the extreme displeasure of the British.

Hamilton's party, the Federalists, was replaced by Jefferson's and Madison's small-government Democratic-Republicans. But Jefferson, Madison, and their successors quickly decided that their small-government, agriculture-first principles had been an out-of-power luxury. So policies to promote industry stayed in place, as did the tariff, rising and falling as political balances shifted. They were augmented by several decades of policies to enable and subsidize canal and later railroad building. And pre–Civil War America, safe from foreign military threat, channeled Department of War money to fund the development of promising high-tech industries at the Springfield Arsenal and elsewhere.

They picked some big winners: one was a way to assemble guns from standardized parts using relatively unskilled labor because America lacked skilled gunsmiths. This innovation shaped far more than America's gun industry; it became the basis for the powerful approach to manufacturing called the *American System*. Tariffs stayed high, and as steel ships radically reduced the costs of transatlantic freight, America raised them still further to effectively offset the impacts of greater efficiency. We didn't even honor the intellectual property of British authors, their copyrights: Dickens was unable to collect royalties on US sales of his best-selling novels.

After Hamilton: Democrats, Whigs, and Republicans

Again and again, America renewed this high-tariff industrialization policy—over the opposition of its farmers and the Southern planters—for the higher purpose of distorting market outcomes in America's favor, protecting its infant industries. It worked very well: the country industrialized at a very rapid pace. By the end of the nineteenth century, those infants had grown to be the largest firms in the world, and America had overtaken free-trade Britain as an industrial power. And it kept those protectionist tariffs, the highest in the North Atlantic, with occasional very short-term drops, right up until World War II.

The nineteenth-century US government took the lead in creating the transcontinental railroads. Railroad expansion reshaped the economy by opening vast regions to profitable farming and settlement and by accelerating the development of feeder industries such as steel and complementary industries such as telegraph. Unforeseeable entrepreneurial industries also developed on the railway, such as the Sears, Roebuck catalog sales, or Swift's meat, which slaughtered out in the Midwest stockyards, not in downtown Boston or Baltimore, and shipped the steaks, not the cattle, east. The government did not tax and spend to do this. It didn't have to. Instead, the government gave railway companies huge tracts of valuable land. Government spending as calculated by national income accountants was a small share of GDP in the nineteenth century. But any government that builds infrastructure and allocates land title on the scale of the nineteenth-century US government is big government incarnate.

The US government even engaged in social design on a big scale. In the mid-nineteenth century, when the federal government sold off millions of acres in what we now call the Midwest, it did not auction the land to the highest bidders. Instead, under the Homestead Act, it entailed the land rights precisely to prevent giant landholdings (and the extension of slavery) and ensure that only a family actually living on and farming the land could get it and hold it. The alternative—an auction, which might now seem the normal and right way to privatize government assets—would likely have resulted in a social structure more like that of Latin America, of very large estates and great masses of landless agricultural laborers, with all its drear consequences.

These were the policies that intelligently designed nineteenth- and most of twentieth-century America. They were pragmatic and concrete in conception—by and large, you would get what you saw—and of course, they were realized with more than just a tiny bit of corruption.

Teddy Roosevelt

The next redesign was the important course correction led by President Teddy Roosevelt. Toward the end of the nineteenth century, giant corporations—*trusts*, as they were then called—came to control their markets rather than being controlled by them. Remedial action began to seem imperative, at least to a great many Americans. If you are to have a private enterprise economy regulated by the forces of market competition, when markets prove unable to regulate themselves—for among other reasons, when firms become too monopolistic—you have three choices: nationalize, regulate, or restore some real degree of competition.

Nationalization, an ideological choice, was off the agenda. So America pragmatically set out to regulate some of the "natural monopolies," such as the all-important railroads, passed antitrust laws to break up some of the most conspicuous unnatural monopolies, such as Standard Oil, and even passed a constitutional amendment establishing the income tax to address the outrageous concentration of wealth of the first Gilded Age.

No revolution; no need for new economic theory to guide or legitimate. A lot of political conflict, yes; but, all in all, a very pragmatic correction to deal with deep structural economic problems.

FDR

When Franklin Delano Roosevelt took office in 1932, the stock market had lost about four-fifths of its 1929 value; the banks were defaulting on their depositors; about half the mortgages in America were in default; about one-third of non-farm workers were unemployed. The New Deal, Roosevelt's wildly pragmatic response to the economic emergency, was the least ideological response of any nation confronting the economic disaster. In many less fortunate lands, ideological solutions from both the left and the right were fought over, usually to the victory of the right, and implemented—to the great grief of their people and neighbors.

The New Deal might be called *pragmatic experimentalism*. The FDR administration tried one thing after another: what didn't work was dropped; what did seem to work was reinforced and expanded. It found its way into almost every corner of the US economy from farms, to bridges and parks, to stock exchanges and banks, to river basins, and to social insurance. It did not focus on opening a new economic space; it initially sought to revive a moribund economy—the first frantic hundred days of the New Deal constituted pre-modern emergency-room resuscitation. This pragmatism, and little else, is what the New Deal shared with the other American redesigns, previous and subsequent.

The New Deal largely imposed its redesigns and as often as not just went forth and implemented them itself. And always quickly: this was emergency action. Never before or since has a peacetime US government commanded and legislated to this extent. It established its own bureaucracies and regulatory authorities: the Social Security Administration; the Securities Exchange Commission, the National Labor Relations Board, the Tennessee Valley Authority (TVA), and the Works Progress Administration (WPA), not to mention the National Recovery Administration, an attempt at industry-led corporatism that was shot down by the Supreme Court. And it hugely and quickly expanded others, such as government mortgage insurance. It taxed and spent, redirecting money flows through the economy at an order of magnitude greater than any peacetime federal government had ever done.

Little of the New Deal was focused, as previous redesigns were, on growing the economic pie in a new direction. Nevertheless, among its very many initiatives were several that clearly tried to open a new economic space for growth, such as the TVA and the huge program of dams in the dry West that opened vast areas for farming, industry, and even cities. The focus was first on overall economic stimulus—recovery, not new capacity. It then turned to issues of security and fairness in the form of farm price supports and subsidies, Social Security, welfare proper, direct employment (as in the WPA and the Civilian Conservation Corps [CCC]), labor unions—the "safety net," as it was later called. It was clearly what the times demanded.

Though the New Deal was not itself ideological but rather the ultimate in pragmatic policy experimentation, it became the definition of the ideology that was post–World War II American liberalism: the regulation of finance, a social safety net, mortgage insurance, high marginal tax rates, and big, active government. It became the model of what government could do and should do.

Dwight D. Eisenhower

After World War II, under Republican president Dwight D. Eisenhower (who defined the center of American politics) and his successors, both Democratic and Republican, it was again government that led the next reshaping of the US economy in four major ways:

First, by preserving the New Deal—the regulation of finance, Social Security, mortgage insurance, infrastructure spending and more generally, big, active government along with high marginal tax rates—over the wishes of a large part of the Republican majority that wanted to dismantle it.

Second, by huge housing and highway programs that promoted a nation of homeowners and enabled the massive suburbanization that drove the economy and reconfigured the physical and the social landscape.

Third, by financing the large-scale development of world-leading research universities, which have been major contributors to the best American economic performance ever since.

Fourth, by directly supporting the development of new technologies, mostly though the huge and now permanent defense budget, American dominance was established in such areas as commercial jet aviation and especially semiconductors, computing, and packet switching, the core technologies of what grew to be the digital era.

This was a big-time exercise in hands-on direction, in deliberate winner-picking, and it was a very big winner for the United States. But it was not a major exception in the history of the US government's involvement in economic redesign, nor was this big-scale effort particularly controversial. Support was broad and deep; opposition, weak. It was concrete economics—what you see is what you'll get. It was not abstract or ideological. It embodied a national sense of where we should be going, what was good and desirable, and what Americans expected their government to do.

There was something for everyone who counted: nice houses with lawns and affordable long-term mortgages for average Americans. These, in turn, necessitated automobiles and highways and refrigerators and washing machines and furniture (which was ideal for the automobile, oil, white goods, home furnishings, and construction industries); a steadily growing and secure market for mortgages and automobile loans; and municipal bonds for infrastructure and schools to please the regulated and respectable finance industry.

Massive and targeted government spending generated the advanced technologies that provided the seed corn for America's continuing technology preeminence. Government involvement did not stifle innovation and entrepreneurship; quite the opposite, it opened to them vast new futures into which they predictably and promptly surged, innovated, and soared.

And American government did not accept ideological handcuffs. When push came to economic shove, the US government even deliberately devalued the dollar in the interest of national economic prosperity. It did so more than once, each party taking a crack: under FDR, under Nixon, and under Reagan. America used all the tools: infrastructure development, tariff protection, direct picking and promoting of winners, exchange rate devaluation, and, during the first Reagan administration, a return to selective protectionism through naked import quotas in the form of "voluntary" export restraints.

The Most Recent Redesign

And then came the most recent redesign, the body sculpting of the US economy by tandem restructuring teams from both East Asian and American governments, which hollowed out the US economy and then flabbed it up.

The East Asian Side

Pioneered by Japan, adopted with significant modifications by Korea and then taken over at system-shattering scale by China, the East Asian nations practiced a Hamiltonian strategy of protecting and fostering industry. This has delivered unprecedented rapid growth by concentrating resources on the production of manufactured goods for export at ever-greater scale, sophistication, and value added, and on gaming the international system of open trade that America was promoting at all costs. They developed a capability for industrial development—a turbo-powered remake of Hamilton's strategy—in which government plays a leading and active role.

The principles were straightforward. Rapid economic development could be achieved only through a massive and sustained movement out of low-productivity peasant agriculture and into industrial production, then continued through an unceasing movement up the value-added chain from low-skill, low-capital, low-wage manufacturing (sewing garments and assembling toys, luggage, trinkets, and shoes) and moving up to higher-capital, higher-skill, and higher value-added industries (steel, shipbuilding, automobiles, and electronics).

Industries were staunchly protected against imports, provided with cheap capital and assisted in obtaining foreign technology. And year after year, government persevered at financial repression, capital channeling, and industrial protection and promotion. Targeted industries focused on exports, since until development had proceeded a very long way, the domestic market—struggling small farmers and subsistence-wage factory workers—was too small, too poor, and too downscale to drive a rapid, massive shift to manufacturing and a long-term climb up the value-added ladder. Only exports could lead the economic reshaping. Every instrument was used, in a roughly coordinated manner, to further this goal—cheap investment finance, protection against imports, zealous and active non-protection of foreign intellectual property, currency manipulation and, when needed, subsidies in various forms and guises.

Is there anything wrong in a government zealously, systematically, and unwaveringly protecting its infant industries against foreign competition and pulling out all the stops to support them; in focusing them on exports; holding down consumption; and reinvesting the proceeds into more and better productive capabilities?

No.

And there is indisputably a lot that is right: it works. The East Asian industrial, high-investment, export-focused economies have grown faster than any in the history of the world (omitting the no-work oil sheikdoms, and perhaps the economy of Wall Street's finance sheikdoms).

But the practice pioneered by the Japanese, exporting more than you import and targeting those exports by industry—first clothes and toys, then steel and ships, then automobiles and machine tools, and then electronics, and doing it at world-impacting scale—means that some other big country (for example, the United States) must import more than it exports year after year, run down its foreign assets, go into debt, and shrink the scale and the incomes in those of its industries targeted by the Asian exporters.

Is there anything wrong with that in terms of the welfare of the world?

No.

More poor people are getting less poor and a much smaller number of richer (but not necessarily rich) people are getting less rich. But that sounds too much like textbook economics, which avoids the question of national borders when speaking of an economy—and the Asian development model is about nothing if not national boundaries.

Right or wrong depends upon whose welfare you are concerned with; that is, unless you feel that the teachings of economics 101 define right or wrong. The textbooks tell us that the operations of a free trade system produce a positive sum game: all sides gain. But in industries of substantial economics of scale, of learning and of spillovers, there is a major zero-sum element to the outcome. Few governments, if any, place the welfare of the rest of the world above that of their own citizens—my gain can well be your loss, and unless things go terribly right, it probably will be.[3]

Industries, often major ones, rise and fall on both sides of the trade relationship less according to classical free market dynamics, and more according to the choice and determination of the nation doing the industrial targeting and the willingness of the government of the targeted industries to permit it. And that is an essential difference from the automatic balances of the classic presentation of free trade and its mutual benefits, where governments do not figure in the equations that have become rather elaborate in recent years. In terms of the structure of production and employment, the gain of one side comes at the expense of the other side, unless—*unless*—the other side (in this case, the United States) can move its resources and people into still higher-value-added activities, industries of the high-value future. Then the game can continue with everyone prospering.

The targeted side of such policies has three choices:

1. It can shift its economy into higher-value-added activities.

2. It can ignore what is happening and simply accept having its economy restructured by the Asian developers.

   or

3. It can refuse to play the game and either dismantle the strategy and apparatus of targeted exports or simply block them.

The United States chose number 1—deliberately shifting to higher-value industries of the future (with a contorted effort to pretend, to the world and to itself, that it was choosing option 2—doing absolutely nothing and letting free markets shape events). Through this bold, but rather furtive policy, it enabled its economy to expand into new, higher-value-added activities. But it made an exceedingly poor choice of which activities.

This body sculpting of America was supposed to move the country into the industries of the future. Poorer people elsewhere were supposed to sew the seams, pour the plastic into molds, snap the pieces together, and bash the metal while we concentrated on the high-value activities. That is how it happened under Eisenhower and his successors: government tolerated a slow shift out of garments, toys, luggage, shoes, and luxury goods and vigorously moved to shift into advanced technologies—commercial aviation, semiconductors, and computers. These were big investments that, for two generations, continued to generate whole new, high-value industries ranging from the high heavens—satellites and all the communication and military applications they enabled—to deep under the sea and earth—using sound waves and advanced computing to locate oil—and through the countless, economy-transforming applications of communications and computing developments that technology companies continue to mine for their commercial applications. And there were many, many others.

That was then.

This time, the industries of the future offered no such richness and produced little in the way of valuable derivative activities. Indeed, it is arguable that they produced nothing (or exceedingly little) of value, serving at the end mostly to redistribute income to the top. The big shift this time was into the processing of real estate transactions, the processing of health-care insurance claims, and especially into finance. As we discuss below, between the mid-1980s and 2009, these industries increased by over five percent of GDP (more than a full Pentagon) to account for just over a twenty percent of GDP. And these obese numbers, as we will see, understate the "real" size of America's chosen growth sectors.

Real estate brokers share a commission, usually six percent of the sale price of a house and the overwhelming majority of houses are sold through brokers. During the prosperous twenty years from 1950 to 1970, with the government-created system of easy mortgage finance functioning smoothly, the average house price rose by about 40 percent—well under 2 percent per year, not even running ahead of inflation. From the mid-eighties to 2006, house prices rose by about 400 percent—and so did brokers' fees. There was no increase in work, service, or real value to the economy: rising returns to real estate transactions were, as economists say, pure rent.

Policy fashioned the grotesque design of the American health-care system, which constitutes about 17 percent of GDP. Compare that with Germany (11.3 percent), France (11.7 percent), Denmark (11.2 percent), or Japan (9 percent)—all of which have older populations and better health outcomes, even if we confine the comparison of outcomes to white Americans. The United States spends over six times more than the OECD average on health-care administration. Over $150 billion are spent every year on the overhead costs and profits of the private health insurance industry, largely to pay for office workers to dispute with workers in other medical offices about which company will pay for medical treatments. The costs must be counted both on the insurance company and on the doctors' office side, where they are probably about another $150 billion a year. Is that real value-added, as treated in the national accounts? Has that particular form of economic growth, that higher-value-added activity of the new US economy, brought any value at all to that economy, or does the work of all those good people just drain value?

Finance was the leading industry to which government opened the growth gates, as it had done previously for manufacturing, railways, suburban housing, and advanced technology. Beginning seriously in the 1980s, government deliberately, piece by piece, dismantled the regulatory structure that had tamed finance into something of a utility. And as in the past, entrepreneurs rushed in and innovated. The lucrative innovations ranged from collateralized debt obligations (CDOs—called by Warren Buffett "financial weapons of mass destruction") and the like, on through high-speed trading (to us, a robotized cousin of front-running).[4]

The increase of the weight of finance in America's GDP came about not so much by increasing the numbers of those employed in the sector, but by increasing the take of those high up in the industry. During the 1970s, average pay in finance was roughly the same as in most other industries; by 2002, it was double.[5] The legions of clerks and tellers remained poorly paid; the gain went to the top, most of it to the top of the top. By 2005, finance accounted for a full 40 percent of all corporate profits. And many of the very most lucrative parts of finance—hedge funds, private equity partnerships, venture partnerships—were not structured and therefore not counted as corporations. Along with the accountants and consultants, add to this profit-making machine the Wall Street law firms that are part and parcel of finance, although they do not count as finance, but rather as business services. Finance got considerably more than 40 percent.

There is no doubt that a country getting its economic policy right—and getting the political economy right so that the country can get its economic policy right—is and has been of overwhelming importance in producing prosperity. And for most of its first two hundred years, the United States did just that—not always easily, not always smoothly, not always cleanly, and decidedly most imperfectly—but all in all, quite successfully.

But beginning in the 1980s, America has been getting its economic policy wrong. For the first time in American history, what government decided to promote and promised as the industries of the future was driven not by pragmatic assessment, but by ideological vision wrapped in abstract economic theories. It was neither pragmatic nor concrete. And, for the first time in American history, the redesign did not work.

Earlier redesigns of the US economy were presented and engineered by government as specific, concrete, and "imageable." Beginning in the 1980s, the US government has not proudly presented in such pragmatic, concrete terms its design for a new economy—light in manufacturing, engineering, and exports, and heavy in finance, health-insurance claims processing, real estate transactions processing, and imports. It has talked instead theoretically, abstractly, of its actions to increase freedom and reduce red tape and rigid regulation by dismantling antiquated restrictions on financial markets and of unleashing the invigorating free play of market forces. Deregulation opened the gates for the economy to surge into finance and out of the areas Asian government policy was so successfully targeting. Because it was the very opposite of concrete economic policy making, the new design enabled policy makers to conceal from the American people—and often from themselves—the likely consequences. And so the country never got to see what it was going to get.

This time, policy makers—and the vast, croaking bog of policy advisers, commentators, opinion leaders, and private-sector power wielders—presented their blinding vision. The government initiatives that led to the new look US economy at the outset of the twenty-first century responded to a vision of how a deregulated global market economy should work. This vision was more than merely ideological; it was positively religious.

This was the pull side: dismantling the barriers, rules, and regulations enabled the metastasizing growth of finance; fighting universal health coverage at all costs enabled the growth of negative-sum health-care administration. This rapid growth produced powerful interests that wholeheartedly support the current configuration of our leading-edge zero-sum and negative-sum sectors, and it supports them. We not only got the economic policy wrong, now we have gotten the political economy wrong—a wrong configuration of power that shapes economic policy.

On the push side, there were Asian governments eager to sell us whatever we want to buy and desperate to promote their own economic development. These are governments that have painfully learned that they cannot afford the ideological indulgence of taking their eye off the ball that is the real economy.

Next

America too must refocus on the real. It is the single most important thing we can do to reboot and reinvigorate our economy, to shift out of ideological incantations and abstract obfuscations and talk concrete economics: Where do we want to go? What will the new economic space look like? Who will inhabit it?

A redesign of the US economy is the policy task as well as the task for economists. The policy debate then becomes a debate about that design and the policy instruments—none perfect, none noncontroversial—to achieve this. And no debate about the country's path forward should be rooted in fairy tales or in theoretical dreams of unfettered markets or in furthering the hollowing-out and flabbing-up body sculpting of the past few decades.

The art of politics is to move the politically possible to overlap the economically sensible. If we look to how the United States repeatedly and successfully transformed its economy, then we must root policy in pragmatism and debate concrete—image-able—designs.

Chapter 1

Alexander Hamilton Designs America

There is an establishment folk wisdom about American history. It is, somehow, never written down in compressed form. So let us try to spell it out:

> America is and has always been Jeffersonian. It is and has been a small-government laissez-faire country, exalting its pioneers, its entrepreneurs, and its small businesses, and deeply distrustful of any sort of "interference" by the government in the economy. In its DNA, America is a country for the self-sufficient and self-reliant, running or at least aspiring to run their own small businesses. Especially suspicious of big government, it greatly prefers a hamstrung version with expressly limited powers only.

This folk wisdom about American history is, to put it bluntly, wrong. It is worth spending a few pages outlining where it is wrong, and then somewhat more pages laying out what history is right.

James Madison did argue vigorously for small government in the 1790s, and it does sound good to many in America today.[1] But it was not convincing to the country even in those 1790s. Instead, it was rejected by comfortable electoral and legislative majorities—and, needless to say, George Washington.

It was not convincing even to Madison's own faction once it had taken the national offices and national power away from the followers of those proponents of a greater government role, John Adams and Alexander Hamilton. Madison certainly did not raise any complaints when it was Thomas Jefferson wielding the powers of the federal government in an expansive manner—by committing the United States to such enterprises as the (beneficial) Louisiana Purchase or the (disastrous) embargo on trade with Europe.

Thus the folk wisdom is simply wrong. Madison may have argued that in allowing then secretary of state Hamilton to establish First Bank of the United States, the federal government was exceeding its mandate. But when Madison was president, he sponsored and signed the bill creating the Second Bank of the United States. Why? Because it would make the country more prosperous. And because, in Madison's eyes, the constitutional issue had been settled; it was "a construction put on the Constitution by the nation, which . . . had the supreme right to declare its meaning."[2]

And was there ever an agricultural operation further from the model of the self-sufficient, self-reliant yeoman than Monticello?

Stepping back, it is clear that the federal government's role in making possible the pioneer farmer whom the Jeffersonians loved was always large. Troops were needed for Indian removal to open land west of the Appalachians to floods of white pioneer farmers. Canals had to be built to transport their crops to market.

The government's role in economic development only grew as the eighteenth century gave way to the nineteenth. In the *Little House on the Prairie* books, author Laura Ingalls Wilder presents a rose-colored view of the self-reliant, end-of-the-nineteenth-century homesteader. But the little house on the prairie in Kansas was a squatter speculation: the hope was that the US Army would remove the native Osage tribe to a new, smaller reservation. Yet for once, the army failed to move an Indian treaty settlement line to make the squatters happy. And so the family moved—forced out, Pa claimed, by big interfering government.

When the Little House family then moved to the Dakota prairie, self-sufficient agriculture was simply impossible. Settlement could not have happened without the world market. Pioneers needed the transportation links to the east and across the Atlantic for two reasons: they needed to sell the staple wheat that they could grow there, and they needed to purchase all the necessities that would not grow in that climate. Without the heavy subsidies for railroad construction to create and maintain those links and the resulting transcontinental and trans-Atlantic division of labor, the Little House family would never have survived *The Long Winter*.[3]

Indeed, government's role in the United States economy in the nineteenth century was far more salient than that of Western Europe's domestic governments of the same era. The United States' infrastructure, military pacification, settlement, internal improvements, research, protectionist tariffs, and market-structuring initiatives had all been crucial to its rapid industrial growth. It was not until the mid-twentieth century that Western Europe's governments began to play a comparable role in their economies.

However, before and during the Revolutionary War era, there was one powerful interest that strongly wanted a "Jeffersonian" small-government America: Britain. Britain did not want a *laissez-faire* global economy. It wanted to shape the global economy to its benefit, and this included preventing the Americans from adopting versions of British policies that would interfere with that shaping.

The claim by John Robert Seely in his 1883 book *The Expansion of England* that Britain had acquired its empire "in a fit of absence of mind" is simply not true.[4] Beginning on November 17, 1558, when Elizabeth I assumed the throne, Britain became a sea power. That was the monarchy's settled strategy. There would be no more attempts at land victories like Agincourt; the lion's share of the armed forces would be deployed at sea and the focus on the potential returns of this control.

And from 1689 on, what John Brewer called the British fiscal-military state was settled policy as well. The willingness of the landlord class to tax itself to support and mobilize a more expensive military than France—which had three times England's population—was historically unprecedented. The British Empire was a project single-mindedly, consciously, and successfully pursued by Britain's military elite. It was, in fact, the most successful such project in Europe since the rise of the Roman Empire two millennia before.[5]

The hope and the reality was that naval dominance would not just protect the island but prove profitable as transoceanic trade and empire brought wealth to Britain. Britain would sell the spices, silks, sugars, cottons, teas, tobaccos, and so forth to continental Europe. It would pay for them in four ways: from the money earned when exporters chose British ships because the British Navy would not sink them, from settler and slave colonies providing rum and sugar from the West Indies, from the taxes and plunder Britain exacted from the rest of its empire, and by exporting higher-value-added manufactured goods back to them and to others. Britain thus imposed control, fees, and commissions on everything going into or out of its colonies. All imports and exports were supposed to pass through Britain, and on British transports. That was the British version of the mercantile system, codified in its navigation acts.

The British were mostly interested in the products of the slaveholding plantations south of the Mason-Dixon line. Applying these controls to non-plantation smallholder colonies in the north was almost an afterthought. But the secretaries of state and their staffs in London had their goals for these colonies as well. All the colonies were supposed to buy from British suppliers only. They were not to make anything that British suppliers sought to export to America. They were to export and import only to and from Britain. The aim of the entire colonial enterprise was to provide Britain with what it wanted cheaply and what it could resell with profit. That meant the northern colonies sold furs and timber to Britain and became a captive market for Britain's goods—plus a dumping ground for its religious recalcitrants and general reprobates.

Of the thirty-five chapters of Adam Smith's 1776 *Inquiry into the Nature and Causes of the Wealth of Nations*, fully eight are devoted to his diatribe against this mercantile system. It was, Smith argued, one in which:

> the interest of the home consumer has been sacrificed to that of the producer ... The interest of our manufacturers has been most peculiarly attended to ... To prohibit a great people [in the colonies] ... from making all that they can of every part of their produce, or from employing their stock and industry in the way that they judge most advantageous to themselves, is a manifest violation of the most sacred rights of mankind ...[6]

Continued British rule would have sent the American economy down a Jeffersonian road designed to please Great Britain's merchants of Bristol. And, once on that road, the natural economic role for the nineteenth-century (and indeed the twentieth-century) United States would have been to spend its energy realizing and building on its comparative advantage in agriculture and resources by importing sophisticated capital- and technology-intensive manufactures from the north of Britain, the industrial heart of the world. It would have paid for them by exporting natural resources and first-stage processed farm, forest, and mining products.

But that was not the way it worked out.

And that is in large part because of the single human being who might be judged to have had the most significant individual impact on the shape of the American economy and its extraordinary growth: Alexander Hamilton. It was Hamilton who set in motion the first and most far-reaching redesign of the American economy.

Republican Virtue or Commercial Prosperity?

Alexander Hamilton: the architect of the boldest, most original and important deliberate reshaping of the economy of the United States of America.

Alexander Hamilton: the only individual who may have been more than the tip of the spearhead of the heavy shaft of an already-thrown, near-consensus view on pragmatic economic policy.

Alexander Hamilton: without whose political-economic interventions, the United States in all probability would not have become the world's second industrial nation, after the United Kingdom.

Alexander Hamilton: major economic theorist. His theory of economic development, first set out in his famous

Report on Manufacturers (1791), not only reshaped America's economy but was channeled by Frederich List half a century later to play a central role in Germany's rapid industrialization, and still later became a canonical text in Japan.[7] It is not core curriculum, or even marginal curriculum in core American and British economics departments. Yet arguably, and we would like to argue it, while Adam Smith's ideas have dominated the textbooks, Alexander Hamilton's ideas have proved more influential in shaping development strategy for the more successful late developers, of which the most prominent have been Germany, Japan, Korea, and now China.

It was not the pioneering and much-studied British approach that guided Germany's rapid industrialization almost a hundred years later, but rather the Hamilton approach as presented in List; then Japan, which borrowed from Germany; then Korea; and now, more than two hundred years after its publication, by China. It has been the preferred route to successful development. Manchester School free-trade, free-market economics has been honored less by successful imitation than by textbook-ization.

Before Hamilton, the Jeffersonian economy—the one that Britain had imposed through its mercantilist colonial policy—was the mold into which America was being poured. After Hamilton, the US economy was different. It was a bet on manufacturing, technologies, infrastructure, commerce, corporations, finance and banks, and government support of innovation. That was the American System of the early nineteenth century.

Hamilton pushed the United States into a pro-industrialization, high-tariff, pro-finance, big-infrastructure political economy, and that push set in motion a self-sustaining process. The economy was then dominated by powerful and durable Federalist and neo-Federalist interest groups that profited immensely from those policies and could more often than not make those policies stick. Representatives of both western farmers and New England manufacturing bosses and workers saw that it was good for them to impose high tariffs on imports of British manufactures bought by grandee Southern slave-owning cotton planters, protect New England's noncompetitive infant industries, and use the tariff revenue to build the infrastructure for an America that would not just be Europe's farmer, logger, and miner, but a manufacturer and a researcher in its own right.

That turned out to be good for more than just farmers and the bosses and workers. It turned out to be good for the country as a whole.

The United States had every chance of sharing the fate of what W. Arthur Lewis called the *economies of temperate European settlement*.[8] Those other countries—Australia, Argentina, Canada, and even the Ukraine—became in the nineteenth century great granaries and ranches for industrial Europe. But none of them developed the industrial base to become fully first-class balanced economies in the late nineteenth century. They obeyed the incentives provided by their then-current comparative advantage. They thus developed extraordinarily productive export agricultural sectors. But that road to what was in the nineteenth century current prosperity also entailed a very heavy and undiversified bet that those trends would continue. When commodity price trends turned against them, they lost relative ground. By contrast, the twentieth century became an American century precisely because America by 1880 was not a gigantic Australia.

Thomas Jefferson believed what he read and had been taught in the schoolroom: 100 BC–100 AD had seen the transformation of Rome from a virtuous farmers' republic into an unfree, overluxurious, corrupt, and bloody empire of plutocrats, moneylender's, proletarians, and slaves. Republican virtue was to be found only in the countryside, where people worked hard and wrested their living from the soil. With military success came the conquest of empire. And with the luxury of imperial conquest and commerce, that republican virtue was lost. Emperor Augustus's wisdom stabilized the situation, but at the price of the Romans' liberty. Thereafter, the best that could be hoped for was the benevolence of wise autocrats like Gibbon's five: Nerva, Trajan, Hadrian, Antoninus Pius, and Marcus Aurelius. But Rome's luck was bound to run out, and it did.

Jefferson saw the British Empire in which he lived as undergoing an analogous historical process, and hence cutting America loose from Imperial Britain as a necessity. It was not that the stamp taxes, arbitrary royal governors, and mercantile system trade restrictions were intolerable. What was intolerable was to be denied the status of self-governing citizens with the liberties of Englishmen and to be forced into the role of subjects of an empire going to imperial hell in a handbasket. But Jefferson had no quarrel with the agrarian economy that the British Empire was designing America to be.

Hamilton, a New Yorker, thought differently. He thought that liberty could spring from the city as well as the countryside. It could be as much threatened by a cohesive block of rural aristocrat-landlords as by the urban mob. It could be guaranteed as much by a society of crossing interests working out their differences for the common prosperity as by an agrarian ideology of self-sufficiency. Moreover, urban commercial prosperity was essential both for a good and a free society. A desperately poor urban population could not be supporters of liberty. A rural society—even one that was frugally prosperous—that lacked a critical manufacturing capability could not defend itself against empire building by Britain, France, the Netherlands, or Spain; at best, it would be dependent on unwanted and unfair foreign alliances.

A generation after Jefferson, President Andrew Jackson clung to the rural American model and consciously echoed Jefferson's egalitarian stance. Jefferson loved the frontier yeoman in the abstract, Jackson in the concrete. Like Jefferson, Jackson's enemies included bankers, corrupt government contractors, and anyone who favored property tests that kept the vote from the (white, male) common people—especially, in Jackson's view, the rural men with their hunting rifles—who Jackson believed had come down the Mississippi at the end of 1814 and enabled him to win the Battle of New Orleans. A Jefferson-Jackson United States would have been rural, Anglo-Saxon, Southern and Border-Southern, and not a technological leader but rather a technological follower.

Jefferson has a grand memorial on the Tidal Basin, and his portrait is engraved on the nickel. A large equestrian statue of Jackson stands in the center of Lafayette Square, across from the White House, and his picture is on the twenty-dollar bill. Alexander Hamilton has only a single statue behind the building that now houses his Treasury Department, and the current secretary of the Treasury wants to remove Hamilton's portrait—and his stern vigilance—from the ten-dollar bill. (Though, we must note that, of all things, a rap musical celebrating Hamilton has become a huge hit.)

Yet today, what we have is not Jefferson-Jackson's but Hamilton's United States of America. And, somehow, in spite of his strong ideological attraction to Jeffersonianism, the policies of Jackson and his Democratic Party—save for the dismemberment of the Second Bank of the United States—were rather more Hamiltonian than Jeffersonian.

Why? Because once the Hamiltonian system was set, it stuck. It worked. And so, very quickly it had become too strong and too useful to too many powerful groups for any Jeffersonian political coalition to dismantle.

The Hamiltonian System

Hamilton's system was constructed of four drivers that reinforced one another, not just economically but politically:

- High tariffs

- High spending on infrastructure

- Assumption of the states' debts by the federal government.

- A central bank

The economy was to be reshaped to promote industry; as noted in the introduction, the aim was not to shift the new and fragile nation's economy to its comparative advantage, but rather to shift that comparative advantage. The principal instrument for this was a high tariff on manufactured imports targeting mostly imports from Britain, the traditional and world-dominant manufacturer. The tariff would provide both the incentive to invest in the development of manufacturing technologies and their build-out. It would also subsidize the nascent manufacturing firms that would make those investments.

The tariff, however, had other goals. It was to be the major source of federal government revenues. A tax on the consumption of imports was overwhelmingly a progressive tax, one that only lightly burdened enterprise, as opposed to the collectors of rents. It would thus support an extensive program of infrastructure development—vital for territorial expansion and economic development—and for adding the critical political support of the western farmers to the northern coastal commercial and labor interests. (And, for those farmers, a government with the resources to field a military force to remove the Indians who stood in their way was worth supporting and even paying for.)

But that was not all. The tariff was also the instrument that permitted the federal government to credibly assume the states' debts incurred to fund the Revolutionary War, thus both strengthening the central government (central to Hamilton's plans) and also paying off very, very handsomely the eighteenth-century version of today's vulture funds, the rich financiers who bought the state debts for pennies of the dollar—and these were, after all, Hamilton's friends.

The creation of a federal government debt also constituted the basis of a new and vigorous financial market (another of Hamilton's goals) and gave the rich (yet another) interest in the survival and success of that government. No wonder that in Hamilton's strong and settled opinion: "a national debt, if it is not excessive, will be to us a national blessing."[9] (The inability of the Eurozone to advance very far in this direction is quite an unhappy contrast: they need a Hamilton in place of their Schäubles, Merkels, and Hollandes, but don't seem to have one in the offing.[10])

Finally there was the Bank of the United States, which Hamilton designed to sit at the center of the financial system, impart solidity, sobriety and control, and tame the wildcat banks and their wildcat currencies.

So, as the Hamiltonian system developed, tariffs rose to about 35 percent of the values of manufactured imports by 1816. And they kept climbing.[11] Added to the very substantial costs of early-nineteenth-century shipping, it was a formidable exercise in manufacturing protectionism, as well as a short-run sacrifice of consumer to producer well-being and static wealth to dynamic technology-based growth.

And up the tariff stayed. It was among the very highest in the North Atlantic for more than a century. When steamships and railroads massively lowered shipping costs, the tariff was boosted up even higher to protect America's infant industries, which were now becoming the biggest in the world. And it stayed up also because for generation after generation, it was popular among those who mattered, those who saw themselves as beneficiaries of growing industry, national infrastructure, and low domestic taxes, and saw that it was good. They did so even though they also found the duties on the manufactured goods they imported from Britain heavy.

It was only after World War II, when the United States assumed its dominant global position and its newfound international responsibilities, did lowering tariffs and moving toward ever-freer trade and greater economic integration of the free world become American policy. By then, America's overwhelming industrial and economic might seemed unchallengeable.

Yet, looking back at economic history, we see country after country that has imposed developmental tariffs and yet failed to develop. A tariff to protect infant industries while filling the federal till can just as well be a national burden as a national blessing. It will be a burden unless those industries do in fact grow up—technologically and organizationally. What is needed is more than just a protective tariff.

Thus, if the Hamiltonian bet was to succeed:

- The opportunities for technological developments that would prove American industry competitive had to be there.

and

- Those opportunities had to somehow be seized.

Seizing the technological opportunities was, as has repeatedly been the case in the United States, from the steamboat to the internet, greatly assisted by federal funding. Department of War money was used to fund the development of promising high-tech industries at the Springfield Arsenal and elsewhere, the pioneers of what would much later be called the *spin-off*. They picked some important winners: the assembly of goods—guns—from standardized and hopefully interchangeable parts, and the use of relatively unskilled labor alongside increasingly skilled machines. The result was the resource-wasting, innovation-forcing approach to high-productivity manufacturing called the *American System*.

America chose not to respect foreigners' intellectual property—and not just in manufacturing. For example, Charles Dickens was unable to collect royalties on US sales of his best-selling novels. Britain would have loved to impose strong intellectual-property protection on nineteenth-century America by negotiating a multilateral partnership (a Trans-Atlantic Partnership that brings to mind the TPP of today). But America would never have considered accepting.

As important as the tariff and state-sponsored theft of intellectual property was the fact that wood, iron ore, and other raw materials, in addition to coal, were dirt cheap in America. Of these, coal alone was as inexpensive in Britain. That meant that in Britain technological development had focused exclusively on that one line of industrial technologies that economized on labor (which was high-priced) and, indeed, on all other inputs—save for hyper-cheap coal. America, by contrast, could easily find the resources to explore all lines of industrial technological development that economized on labor alone.

It should thus be no surprise that there were, among America's broad technological portfolio, lines of technological development that ultimately proved superior domestically. And after sufficient development, they proved superior even in manufacturing strongholds like Britain, where wood, ore, and other inputs remained expensive.

Britain protected non-landed property from politics to a remarkable degree, focusing its tax system on consumption excises and land. It had its engineering culture. Even so, why were the first-generation technologies developed in Britain? Why were they not developed in, say, (somewhat richer) eighteenth-century Holland or perhaps in first-century Alexandria? They were developed in Britain because they were not profitable to deploy anywhere outside of Britain. Britain had both uniquely cheap coal and uniquely high real wages. These wages had been produced by Britain's mercantile-imperial domination of the oceans. The low price of coal delivered to the boiler was the result of geography, yes. But the country's technology development was also the result of other important factors, including, the political economy of parliamentary supremacy, the merchant-gentry electorate, and eminent domain, all of which made it impossible to block the coal-mining/canal-transport complex once the gentry who elected the members of Parliament got the scent of money in their nostrils.

Thus the first-generation industrial technologies developed in eighteenth-century Britain had been designed for late-eighteenth-century British factor proportions and late-eighteenth-century British factor prices. Indeed, the first-generation industrial technologies were not profitable to deploy much of anywhere outside of Lancashire.

But fast-forward several technological generations. The third-generation versions of the British-developed spinning and weaving and power and iron technologies developed by the mid-nineteenth century were highly profitable to deploy in the Ruhr, in Belgium, in New England, and elsewhere in Britain than in those parts that were both high-wage and accessible to water transport. And the fifth-generation versions developed by the end of the nineteenth century were profitable to deploy anywhere the market and the politics would allow.

The same thing is true of the American technologies developed as a result of the Hamiltonian system. The first-generation, mid-nineteenth-century versions were too wasteful of raw materials wood and ore to be employed even in Britain. Remember, the only thing super-cheap in Britain was coal, so since labor did not have the option of "lighting out for the territory," it was better to economize on wood and ore by employing more labor. But the third-generation early-twentieth century versions of these American technologies were profitable to deploy even in Britain. And the fifth-generation versions of the age of Fordist mass production were profitable to deploy everywhere.

The "interchangeable parts" claims were overstated—Eli Whitney was creating his own personal reality-distortion field when he promised the US Department of War things he could not deliver. But the rest was solid: even though Britain had been the home of the Industrial Revolution for 150 years— ever since the first steam engines had been built to suck water out of coal mines so London could get its fuel—and even though Britain at mid-nineteenth century had 2.5 times the people and four times the number of engineers of the United States, the principal locus of innovation had already moved.

Thus even before the US Civil War, the Hamiltonian system and its success were seen as alarming on the eastern side of the Atlantic. British parliamentary investigating committees were convened. They puzzled over the conundrum: How was it that America had developed technologies that somehow gave their manufacturers higher profits, paid their manufacturing workers higher wages, and enabled greater ease of repair through interchangeable parts than did British technologies? This Hamiltonian project was contrary to Ricardo's canons of comparative advantage as well as Smith's free markets. It was bold. The direction of economic activity was not commanded, but it was not left unguided either. It was directed—what the French would later call *dirigiste*: the government would offer to support industrial development, and even though the offer *could* be refused business found itself not wanting to. Even though it was not free-market or in accord with America's then-apparent comparative advantage, in retrospect it was not un-smart. Indeed it was the smartest intelligent design of all. It brought to the world technological and organizational innovations of enormous value:

- The American System of interchangeable parts

- Fordist mass production

- The Chandlerian bureaucratic corporation

- Government support for industrial research, which was to become the true late twentieth-century game changer

To say that American industrial technologies were "just" the result of different factor proportions and costs, and not a qualitative change like the British Industrial Revolution, is to mistake the nature of the Industrial Revolution. It is not a process of picking out of a book of known blueprints those technologies that fit your factor proportions and factor scarcities. It is a process, rather, of continuous exploration and innovation—and then rapid spread and further development of those ideas that turn out, when implemented, to be most productive and most useful.

These benefits were massive. They were also massively unexpected. Hamilton believed that a focus on manufacturing, technology, secondary-product exports, corporate organization, banks, and finance was a very good bet. He and his allies had no idea how good a bet it would be. Nobody did. Adam Smith certainly did not. The first who did came in subsequent generations: Charles Babbage and his contemporaries and then, half a century after Hamilton, Karl Marx and Friedrich List and theirs. But even they would have been surprised. And there was no way to predict which would be the best technologies and what their benefits would be in the long run; only experimentation would reveal these.

The classical and neoclassical economics argument—that there is a better development policy in theory—remains true, though it has always been unclear about the borders of an economy: a nation or an international economy. For policy makers, there is no more important difference. If powerful productive economies come from growing organizations that can produce at scale and from growing engineering innovations that generate engineering-practice spillovers, subsidizing efficient large-scale organizations and efficient engineering innovations is better than bluntly taxing manufactured imports.

But efficiently subsidizing only those efficient organizations and spillover-generating innovations would require a policy scalpel. And the only tool the government has at its disposal is a broad axe. There is no better way of determining which organizations and engineering communities deserve and can efficiently use subsidies than to provide them with enough protection that they can try to export, and watch which ones successfully do so.

Economists by their training work under the assumption that all changes shift a stable market equilibrium of countervailing forces in equipoise. Countervailing forces pushing from that direction will strengthen in response to the strength of a shift, and damp the ultimate effect to a small displacement from the initial equilibrium. Thus any shift in any direction is likely to be minor. We are far less confident in that assumption.

We see enormous gaps in relative prosperity emerging in the Industrial Age. In 1500, the world's economic leaders in prosperity and population density were in Asia. Between 1740 and 1970, the ratio of relative material prosperity between them and the North Atlantic fell from 1:2 to 1:30. And the Industrial Age saw the United States open up a 2:1 productivity advantage vis-à-vis other economies that seemed in the early nineteenth century, and seem today, equally blessed by natural environment, the luck of history, and political culture. We see this productivity gap pulling in immigrants at a pace that doubles population density relative to other early twentieth-century New World economies. We see a twentieth century that was not a British, a North Atlantic, or an Anglospherian, but an American century.

We find it very difficult to understand this as an inevitable equilibrium phenomenon, destined for accomplishment whether Alexander Hamilton survived to become America's first Treasury Secretary, or had been killed by a chance cannonball when he fought in the Yorktown Campaign.

Once the Hamiltonian system had been launched, it proved remarkably durable in spite of the political triumphs of factions that loathed it on an ideological level.

Consider the political career of Andrew Jackson. The Democratic Party he founded is still animated by his principle of extending the suffrage and letting the common people—rather than Federalist, planter, merchant, or Whig elites—speak and rule, and his distaste for entitled, trust-funded elites.[12] But Jackson's attempt to wrestle the course of American economic development away from the hands of merchants and manufacturers and canal builders and bankers was unsuccessful. His partisans and partisan successors had abandoned even the attempt to put it into effect before he was dead. The Hamiltonian System made so much pragmatic sense—for most.

It is true that the Hamiltonian tariff was a source of displeasure for British exporters. It was also strongly opposed by those, largely on the coastal South, who were heavy buyers of foreign-made manufactured goods. From "Tariff of Abominations" rates of over 50 percent in 1828, tariffs would fall somewhat whenever Southern Democrats could tip a legislative coalition. The Walker Tariff of 1846 reduced average rates to 23 percent, and the Tariff of 1857 further reduced them to 17 percent. But with representatives from the Confederacy absent from Congress during the Civil War, the tariff rate went back up quickly: the Morrill Tariff (1861) jumped average rates back to 33 percent. They were still about as high in 1900. And the high-tariff policy did not breathe its last until after Smoot-Hawley in 1931.

Martin van Buren and Jackson's other lieutenants and successors at the head of the pre–Civil War Democratic Party did not share Jackson's practical-Jeffersonian love of frontier yeomen. They did not share his hatred of national banks and eastern elite merchants. For them, it was just red meat for the base. But even if they had shared it, they would have put policies to implement it on the back burner. There was little electoral percentage to it.

Americans in the West needed canals, roads, an army to effect the removal of native tribes—and then taking even more, stealing one-third of the value of agricultural land in North Carolina from the Cherokee by unjudicial process long after the military frontier had passed to the west—and the Army Corps of Engineers to dredge and stabilize the rivers. Americans in the Northeast needed the cheapest possible communication with the West—their market and also their source of natural resources—and needed the tariff shield against the then more efficient British manufacturers in order to prosper. And of course, the Hamiltonian tariff was the major source of federal government revenues.

Small-scale white farmers in the South wanted to appropriate the Cherokee land. White farmers north and south also wanted their children to have the opportunity to move west. The planters of the South saw themselves as the big losers under the Hamiltonian system. The heavy tariff forced them to buy either inferior products from New England or to fund the federal Treasury. But Hamilton's system also delivered for them: they had the same material interest in communication and transport links as other Americans seeking prosperity, and as soil exhaustion set in near the East Coast, they had an even greater interest in expansion into the new slaveholding territories of Florida, Texas, Missouri—and the prospect of future expansions into the Caribbean.

When the chips were down, even the planters needed a federal government strong enough for imperial expansion and manifest destiny and also strong enough to curb antislavery agitators in the North. They thus needed enough Northern political allies to make sectional peace a national political priority—which meant that smart Southern politicians found themselves bidding for national votes, and the best way to do that was as supporters of the Hamiltonian system.

Thus Hamiltonian policies flourished under a Jacksonian cloak of hard cider, universal (white male) suffrage, and the rhetorical exaltation of the riflemen of Kentucky.

––––––––––

The last necessary component of the economy that Hamilton wished to create was for the government to build up finance.

For Hamilton, the financialization of the American economy was not to be an end but merely a means. It was good that America's rich—even those who had simply become rich recently through successful debt speculation—be heavily invested in the success of the country by virtue of their holding valuable federal rather than wastepaper state bonds. That the return of British rule would carry financial loss for America's rich was another blessing bestowed by a national debt. And of course, people with talent or ideas needed to be somehow matched with people with money so that commerce and manufactures could grow: the core role of high finance.

The first step in jump-starting the financial market necessary to support such matching was to get America's rich used to buying and selling securities via a thick market in US government bonds. The second step would be to establish a national bank to serve as a clearinghouse. "Wildcat" as an economic term originated not in the oil but in the banking industry. And originally it was not a compliment. If you tried to pay with a banknote printed by a "wildcat bank," the fear was that the bank was so far out on the frontier that wildcats had eaten the bankers and there was nobody left alive to stand behind the note. The goal was a banking system that was large and rich, but even more so, controllable and stable.

The point was not to create go-go financial princes on Wall Street. The point was rather to bind the wealthy to the success of the federal government, and to the success of the commercial and industrial enterprises that would spring up as a result of federal assumption of the debt, federal creation of the bank, and the resulting deepening of financial markets.

Through all this Hamilton explained, eloquently and perceptively, the benefits of his policies to promote commerce, banking, and industry. Hamilton advocated for assumption of the national debt, for a national bank, for federal government encouragement of manufactures, for an army and a navy and domestic industries to equip and supply them, for internal infrastructure improvements, and for a tariff-based tax system to finance them and protect the infant industries from cheaper and better imports.

From the Hamiltonian System to Mass Production

The Hamiltonian system did stick. It flourished, and slowly transformed itself first into the American System of manufactures and then into mass production and Fordism proper. And it set the pattern for all subsequent redesigns of the American economy. These too have involved an analogous seedy inter play of interests and compromises on what government could do to enable growth, and how it should do it.

Politicians have created policies; policies have created interests; interests have entrenched themselves.

And so, when the political wheel turns, politicians who had opposed the policies of industrial development and economic redesign when out of office find that sharply breaking with them would impose too great a strain on their own coalition.

Initiated by governments of one party, the initiatives of the developmental state have then been sustained by governments of the opposite party.

Economists, when they think about it, have tended more often than not to attribute the alternative technological path followed by US engineering and manufacturing in the nineteenth century to the immensely "wasteful" use of the country's abundant natural resources in production. This waste, they tend to say, was economically efficient for America, given the extraordinary ample supply and remarkably low cost of natural resources. They are likely to see America's engineers and manufacturers not so much developing new, different, and simply better technologies as simply making different choices from a book of blueprints.

But none of the other economies of temperate European settlement developed equivalent edges in resource-using manufacturing technologies in their nineteenth centuries— or, indeed, did much to match US methods of productivities. They continued to use British manufacturing technologies, in large part because they continued to draw their engineers from Britain. The biggest benefits of the Hamiltonian system lay not so much in pulling technologies out of a book of blueprints that were more suited in the long run for America's factor proportions and factor costs. The biggest benefits came from the exploration of technological possibilities in the first place.

So the Hamiltonian bet turned into the American System, which was expected by some. And that turned into mass production proper, which was expected by few, if any. And that has since spread over an ever-increasing proportion of the globe. It was an American system—not a Canadian or Argentinean or Australian system, let alone a Ukrainian system. Yet all these countries are places with similar claims to an extraordinarily low ratio of the price of resources to the price of even semiskilled and semiliterate manufacturing-suited labor. Natural resources cheap enough and abundant enough to allow for their immensely wasteful use in production were necessary for manufacturing power, but far from sufficient. What turned out to have been needed was a government to support its development.

What was needed, and what the United States got at the right time, was Alexander Hamilton.

Chapter 2

Additional Redesigns

FROM LINCOLN TO FDR

The conventional history of Lincoln and his mid-nineteenth-century Republican Party focuses on what is by far most important. Ending slavery. Preserving the United States. The Civil War.

But there was more. There was also economic redesign.

Hamilton and his followers did not set the economic framework once and for all and then consign the shape and fate of the economy evermore to the market—the market as they had built it with tariffs, support for transportation infrastructure, high finance, and subsidies for interesting technologies like interchangeable parts—so major redesigns have followed ever since.

In the era of Lincoln and his Republican successors redesign was launched around free labor. As historian Eric Foner has long stressed, the pre–Civil War Republican ideology was not simply that slavery was evil, it was that free labor was very good—and that free labor deserved all possible government support.[1] It deserved support first and foremost via the restriction of slavery to where it currently existed, second by placing the institution of slavery on the road to ultimate extinction, and third—once military necessity aligned with moral imperatives and overrode adherence to the constitutional bargain of 1789—emancipation and citizenship. But it also deserved support via the rejection of the Know-Nothing "American Party" demands for a restriction of immigration. It deserved support via the Homestead Act—free soil. And there was more: free education via the establishment of public land-grant universities; and also free corporations—new legal, financial, and business structures, to accommodate and further enable the new reality of American business with rapid increase in size and importance of industrial firms, of which the biggest and most systemically important were, of course, the railroads.

Nineteenth-century Republicanism was a set of economic policies, as well as the more-important anti-slavery policy. Or, rather, a set of economic policies as appropriate complements and extensions—for what is the anti-slavery position but the ultimate free-labor economic policy? It aims not just at freeing the slave—transferring ownership of human capital from the slaveholder to the self—but also at making that ownership of one's self real by changing labor-market bargaining power. As long as slavery is a living social institution, workers who are not themselves slaves find themselves competing in a labor market set by slave wages. Freeing slaves meant freeing labor.

Lincoln and his Republican successors doubled down on Hamilton's project. They strengthened commitment to the tariff. The federal government did need revenue: save for the Civil War period, the tariff had been and would be its major source of funding until the ratification of the income-tax amendment in 1913. Nevertheless (as noted in chapter 1), the Hamiltonian industrialization-spurring tariff had been in slow decline in the generation between Andrew Jackson and the Civil War—from 50 percent in the 1828 "Tariff of Abominations" to 23 percent in 1846. But, with representatives from the Confederacy absent from Congress during the Civil War, the tariff rose quickly, to 33 percent in 1861 and then back to 50 percent. And for more than a generation after the war ended, Southern representatives—after the end of the First Reconstruction in 1877 almost invariably Democrats, because the Republicans had freed the slaves—were not members of the Republican governing coalition. Thus a legislative block to raising rates of protection was removed whenever Republicans were the congressional majority. And there was only one Democratic president between James Buchanan, elected in 1856, and Woodrow Wilson, elected in 1912. Thus high tariffs became even more central to American governance as one of the core planks of Republican economic policy—just when American manufacturers, no longer the infant industries of Hamilton's generation, were becoming the biggest and most powerful in the world.

In the post–Civil War generation, as steam ships and railways lowered the huge costs of international shipments, America pushed up the tariff rate to offset the efficiency gains of the new technologies. America was now the protectionist exception in a world suddenly seized by the liberal ideas of freer trade and lower tariffs. 1860 to 1879 was precisely the time when European tariffs were reduced. In 1860 France began following England's early example by lowering its tariffs; by 1875, average French tariffs were between 12 and 15 percent; for the Netherlands, 3–5 percent; for Germany 4–6 percent; for England 0 percent.[2] For the United States, the rate was 50 percent.[3]

In nineteenth-century America, high tariffs proved politically popular (outside the South, which was still largely out of the game). When Grover Cleveland made tariff-reduction his principal reelection campaign issue in 1888, he lost—returning to the presidency in 1892 only after focusing on other issues. In turn, the chief tariff raiser, William McKinley, of the 1890 McKinley Tariff, rode this legislative accomplishment, into the presidency in 1896. And the United States stayed the high-tariff nation up until World War II, when it switched roles to become the world's free-trade leader.

Hamilton's project had called for hefty investment in infrastructure. In post–Civil War America, infrastructure meant railroads. By the end of the nineteenth century, a staggering 200,000 miles of track had been laid (five times the current length of interstate highways). All were privately owned. All were privately run. And almost all were, in one way or another, publicly subsidized. One way to subsidize was simply to grant public lands to railroads in return for construction: 180 million acres of public land were gifted to railroads—281,000 square miles, the equivalent of a square more than five hundred miles on a side, a territory several times the size of England. But this was better than a big square, as all the land along the railway was prime. This was truly a sovereign gift.

Nineteenth-century railroads reshaped America to an extent unapproached previously, and perhaps since. They connected the East. They opened up the West. They generated new farms, mines, factories, and cities. They drove vast increases in output, quality, and productivity for their major supplier industries—for the burgeoning American steel industry, which soon became the biggest in the world, and for the coal and machinery industries. They also fueled the need for more and more and more labor, increasingly imported. They made possible huge increases in scale and efficiency in a host of other industries and also in agriculture, where they enabled 250 percent gains in productivity in wheat to find markets. And just as the opening of a new economic space should, the railroad space generated innovation after innovation—even unanticipated apps.

Sears, Roebuck & Co., an early railroad-enabled app, offered through its printed catalog just about everything a farm—or town—family could desire, or even imagine. Fill in the order form and whatever you wanted would be delivered on the Post Office railcar; pay your pal at the local post office when you picked it up. Clever business model. Sears grew to be the world's largest retailer for the better part of a hundred years. The railroads enabled myriad new businesses, and many quickly became giants: witness Swift & Company, which first had the idea of butchering cattle near the railroad junction in Chicago (inventing the dis-assembly line, the precursor of Ford's assembly line), then loading steaks and chops into refrigerated rail cars and delivering them, rather than live cattle, to New York, Boston, and Baltimore.

America's railroad hyper build-out was corrupt, yes. Wasteful, yes. Outrageous, yes. But the great post–Civil War doubling down on railroad subsidies was essential to create the continental market on which American entrepreneurs were to build the high-throughput, high-economies-of-scale, mass-production industries that made America, as Leon Trotsky later remarked "the furnace where the future was being forged."[4]

The railroads eliminated local monopolies—the friendly producers or merchants in towns who sold goods at low volume and high prices—and replaced them with the greater variety of the lower-cost, higher-standard-quality goods mass-produced by national-scale monopolies.

The revolutionary impacts of the railroads did not stop at the ocean's edge. Teamed with steel-hulled steamships, they made Midwestern grain at the port of Bremen, Germany, cheaper than Prussian rye, creating the crisis that opened the way for Bismarck's "marriage of rye and iron," the political-economy base of Germany's rapid industrialization.

Free Corporations

Today we have little sense of how extraordinary the coming of the new corporation—especially the large industrial corporation—was in the context of laissez-faire, private-property capitalism as an ideology, as an accustomed set of rules, and as a society. The modern corporation is defined by an exorbitant privilege: its owners do not have to pay its bills. The maximum that individual shareholders can be assessed in total for the corporation's debts, no matter how spectacular its bankruptcy, is the value of their shares. The value of equity falls to zero, and the shareholders walk away. All other assets of the owners are safe; the creditors of the corporation can reach only the resources that are kept within the corporate veil.

This doctrine of limited liability is a striking restriction on creditors' rights and on the value of their private property— the debt that they hold. Its purpose is pragmatic: industrial development required that equity financing be raised on a large scale from a great many people. But very few of the investors either wanted or were capable of the kind of close engagement in the affairs of the companies traditionally borne by partners who were jointly and severally liable for all the debts of the enterprise. They wanted only a shot at the gains and no liability beyond the value of their shares. And so it is today. On top of this privilege, the post–Civil War era Republican ascendancy added others: corporations were no longer seen as organizations with a semi-public purpose, with the terms of their charters restricting what they could and could not do. Instead, they became virtual "persons"—with the same due process rights to protect their life, liberty, and property as citizens of the United States. Republican judges made law, then codified by Republican legislators, that these exorbitant privileges of limited liability, unrestricted range of activity, and legal personhood extend beyond the grave of corporate bankruptcy to debtor-in-possession reorganizations under what we now call Chapter 11. This new, artificial, and unprecedented legal structure was a pragmatic response to the scale, complexity, and, especially, the importance of big, industrial firms. Auctioning off the assets on the courthouse steps, the traditional way of wrapping up bankruptcy in an economy of small units of personal property, just would not do for ever-more giant, ever-more systemically important firms. And the biggest (some employed tens of thousands), the most complex, and by far the most systemically important were the railroads. They were also the source of frequent financial blowups. High-rolling financiers repeatedly bankrupted railroads as they fleeced creditors and shareholders (especially English investors, who kept pouring money into the biggest of the next big thing). The new legal structure kept the trains running; and the trains kept the economy going.

All this constituted an extraordinary redefinition of private property undertaken not on the basis of ideology or theory, but pragmatically, in response to profound changes in economic structures and institutions. The corporations were not too big to fail, but they were definitely too big, and too important, to shut down. A big-business economy just can't operate very well under the rules and controls of a small business market system.

The new free corporation was not the only change in laws and regulations that would soon be needed to adapt a market economy to the new scale of its productive units, but those other changes were more contentious and came on in political fits and starts a bit later.

Free Soil

Once the Southerners had left the Congress in 1861, and before the Emancipation Proclamation was issued, the Republican Party passed the Homestead Act (1862), which allowed anyone twenty-one or older (or head of a household if younger) who had never taken up arms against the United States to file an application for a homestead of 160 acres of federal land, live on and improve the land for five years, and take title essentially for free. The measure served to keep slavery out of the territories. But even after the Civil War, when slavery was no longer an issue, homesteading was extended several times to new territories. Eventually, over 1.5 million homesteads were granted, totaling some 270 million acres. This was a grand exercise in social design, implementing Jefferson's vision of a nation of independent farmers—of yeomen, not laborers. And it was fundamentally and deliberately different from what today is generally considered to be the normal and right way to dispose of government assets: sell them to the highest bidder. Auctioning off the Midwest to the highest bidders would likely have resulted in a society very like that of old Russia or Latin America, huge landholdings and a population of farm laborers—the opposite of free and independent farmers. Faint echoes of the social design of the Homestead Act reverberated almost a hundred years later, when America by design staked millions of Americans to a freestanding, freehold house on the urban fringe—what became mass suburbanization.

In addition to "Vote Yourself a Farm," the Republicans offered, "Vote Yourself an Education." In 1862, again in the absence of Southern congressmen and senators, they passed the Morrill Act of 1862. Also known as the Land Grant College Act, it opened the way for smart young Americans to acquire another kind of valuable property: a college education at a new land-grant university. This too, was an exercise in social planning and, like the Homestead Act, was picked up about a hundred years later, when the GI bill sent thousands of returning soldiers to college at the government's expense. And this too contributed in important ways to a more productive economy and a better-informed, more independent, more responsible citizenry.

And the Republican ascendancy backed immigration. Their most important paymasters wanted lots of immigrant labor. The railroads needed laborers by the tens of thousands for tough and dangerous work on their enormous build-out; they also needed settlers to monetize the millions of acres of land they had been given and to have something to carry on those tracks. The ever-bigger industrial firms and coal mines needed low-cost, disciplined labor, and a workforce divided by language and nationality, they felt, was particularly useful in keeping wages down and labor from organizing. (The Republican ascendency from the legislators down through their appointed judges did not at all like the idea of labor organizing. They were true-blue on the side of the big industrialists when they confronted efforts by their workforce to organize and demand better pay and better working conditions.) The big city bosses also needed the new immigrants, whose votes they would quickly obtain and keep, and many recent immigrants wanted family and friends from the old village to come and join them. There were also many in the Republican leadership who liked the idea of knowing that they were the party of opportunity, especially when opportunity was the chance to work hard.

In the 1850s, the Know-Nothing base of what was to become the Republican Party was almost as opposed to immigrants (who they feared would move into their territories and states) as they were opposed to slavery. And, come the 1920s, the gates of immigration to America were to be largely shut by a moral panic that overwhelmed the political voice of both employer and immigrant community interests. While the worthies of the Republican Party who employed immigrants in factories or who rented apartments to immigrants in cities surely gained massively from the open gates of America from the mid-1860s to the mid-1920s, the average Republican voter probably did not. But most Americans were neither slaves, nor bosses hiring labor, nor hired labor. These were the Americans who voted most, and in the end their view of their material and moral interests overrode the seamless fabric of Republican-Party ideology in this respect, and shut down immigration.

As Abraham Lincoln had put it 1861:

There is no such . . . thing as a free man being
fixed for life in the condition of a hired laborer . . .
A large majority belong to neither class—neither
work for others nor have others working for them.
In most of the Southern States a majority of the
whole people of all colors are neither slaves nor
masters, while in the Northern a large majority
are neither hirers nor hired . . . Many independent
men everywhere in these States a few years back
in their lives were hired laborers. The prudent,
penniless beginner in the world labors for wages
awhile, saves a surplus with which to buy tools or
land for himself, then labors on his own account
another while, and at length hires another new
beginner to help him. This is the just and generous and prosperous system which opens the way
to all, gives hope to all, and consequent energy
and progress and improvement of condition to all.
No men living are more worthy to be trusted than
those who toil up from poverty; none less inclined
to take or touch aught which they have not honestly earned . . .[5]

The overall thrust of post–Civil War economic-redesign
policies was seen as pragmatic and American. That this is
the case is shown most obviously by how much those who
opposed these Republican policies hoped to gain from the
election of a Democrat to the presidency in the days of
Republican Party ascendancy, how hard they found such

an election to be in the days of Grant, Hayes, Garfield, and Arthur, and how little policy did change with Democrat Grover Cleveland's first election in 1884, his supersession by Republican Benjamin Harrison in 1888, and Cleveland's second election in 1892. It was not a Republican but Cleveland who vindicated the rights of property and enterprise by attaching a mail car to every train, in order to make Pullman strikers guilty of the federal crime of interfering with the mail and who sent troops into Illinois over the objections of the state's governor, John Peter Altgeld.

If any additional clue to the consonance of pragmatic Gilded-Age Republican economic policies was needed, it was given by the catastrophic defeat suffered when the Democrats nominated a candidate from the Populist wing of the Democratic Party. William Jennings Bryan, the boy orator of the River Platte, might roar, most famously against those who opposed the free-silver plank of his platform:

> If they dare to come out in the open field and
> defend the gold standard we will fight them to
> the uttermost . . . You shall not crucify mankind
> upon a cross of gold.

The elites were indeed fearful of Bryan. But, in the end, the white, male electorate did not buy it. Property, enterprise, education, opening natural resources, immigration, government support of businesses aiming at technological progress and economies of scale—the most that any coalition would deviate from that was the Progressive-movement course correction of Theodore Roosevelt.

Theodore Roosevelt and the Progressive Movement

The young, pre-presidential Theodore Roosevelt talked the talk of a member in good standing of the Republican ascendancy of the post–Civil War generation. He denounced what we would now see as very small files to smooth down some of the roughest edges of the late nineteenth century Gilded Age as if they were pikes of advancing communism—indeed, his denunciations of Democratic 1896 presidential candidate William Jennings Bryan as a puppet of foreign-born Communists sound as though they could come from some Tea Party rally of today:

> [William Jennings Bryan] would be as clay in the hands of the potter under the astute control of the ambitious and unscrupulous Illinois communist [Governor John Peter Altgeld] . . . free coinage of silver . . . but a step towards the general socialism which is the fundamental doctrine of his political belief . . . He seeks to overturn the . . . essential policies, which have controlled the government since its foundation . . . [6]

Roosevelt was strong on the tariff. But once in the presidential seat, put there unexpectedly and to the discomfiture of the Republican old guard by President McKinley's assassination in 1901, Theodore Roosevelt the "wild man," sang a new song. Out went the old Republican ideology and abstractions. In came pragmatic, practical, and concrete change to tame the most flagrant abuses of the new monopoly-led, robber-baron economy. President Roosevelt was keenly aware that markets were imperfect devices; that malefactors of great wealth could warp them to destructive ends; and that giving too much power to government ran the risk of enriching corrupt political machines that did not produce but rather hobbled America. But he also knew that too much power in the hands of the rich had analogous bad effects. The balance of forces had to be reset.

Roosevelt in office was happy to make deals with Populists and Democrats. He put himself at the head not so much of the Republican Party as of a progressive coalition. And, when he thought the stakes were high enough, he was even willing to split the Republican Party and throw the presidential election of 1912 to sort-of-progressive Democrat Woodrow Wilson rather than see his own protégé and chosen successor, Republican William Howard Taft, win a second term. Taft, he thought, had become too much the prisoner of the moneyed interests of his day. And that, he thought, was not a path forward for America.

The currents of progressivism were harnessed, not created by Roosevelt and Wilson. At the end of the nineteenth century, America's WASP political elite had reached a near-consensus that five political dysfunctions showed that the post–Civil War economy had somehow gone awry, and that another government-led economic redesign was needed to correct the course.

First, out on the prairies, both on the farms and in the mines, there were the Populists. The Populists denounced deflation, price-gouging by railroad monopolies (which were

the only way to ship the harvest east), wage-gouging by mining monopolies (the only potential employers in towns whose
promises of high wages had induced people to move hundreds
if not thousands of miles to reach), and the high interest rates
of tight money and deflation that made the burden of paying
off farm debts unbearable. Under these economic pressures,
the elite near-consensus thought, the people of the prairies
were losing their nerve, their work ethic, and their confidence
in the United States, and the social fabric was unraveling as
they succumbed to rum. It was, they thought, necessary to
buck the people up.

Second, new immigrants were pouring into cities in
waves that were too large to be assimilated rapidly. Corrupt
urban machines, rather than healthy town-meeting democracy, resulted. The new immigrants, it was thought, were
not becoming Americans fast enough, perhaps because they
included too many who were too alien and too subnormal
in genetic intelligence—like the Irish, the Italians, the Jews,
and the Slavs. And too many were still attached to the Roman
Catholic Church, which did not teach self-reliance, diligence
in one's calling, and the Protestant work ethic.

Third, there was the ex-Confederate South: defeated in the
Civil War, still largely illiterate, still ruled by an oligarchy that
stifled development, and resolutely poor and backward. This
bloc had, with the disenfranchisement of the Negro, become
the solid Democratic South.

Fourth there were the trusts, the gigantic monopolistic corporate combinations financially engineered by J. P. Morgan
and others—the steel trust, the tobacco trust, the Standard Oil

trust, the sugar trust, the match trust, the shipping trust, not to mention the railroads. Markets could not control them; they controlled their markets. Something new was needed, some countervailing forces or institutions to restore balance and preserve a private market economy and the advantages of mass production and distribution.

And finally, with the trusts came the income distribution of the Gilded Age, the vast accumulations of conspicuous wealth—something America has recently recreated—that ran outrageously counter not just to Jefferson's vision of America (if not his actual life) but even to Hamilton's.

The crushing power of the trusts, the confiscation of the nation's wealth by their owners, the unraveling of the social fabric on the prairie and its reflection in Populism, the failure of the social fabric to knit up among the new immigrants in the cities and its reflection in the corrupt urban machines, the failure of the South to educate itself and rejoin America and its reflection in its solid vote against the party of Lincoln—"Rum, Romanism, and Rebellion" in the words of the Reverend R. B. Burchard in 1884—were the signs that America's economy needed another redesign.[7] And so the Progressive movement was born.

Some Progressives thought that the right road forward was to identify with and tame the forces that were driving the Democratic Party: turn populist and Southern discontent in properly technocratic directions and harness the smarter of the machine politicians of the cities to good-government measures to boost their urban economies—for a machine boss saw himself as having as huge an interest in successful urban economic development as anyone. Others thought that the Republican Party was their natural home as the natural political heart of America—but that it needed to be recognized and that it took social Darwinism and Herbert Spencer's *Social Statics* too seriously—that America needed a market economy but not a market society.[8] All Progressives were willing to work across party lines, for it was the cause of redesigning the American economy rather than partisan advantage that was the true prize.

And so, in fits and starts between 1890 and 1925, the bulk of the Progressive agenda was gradually put into place. In monetary policy, accepting the Populist demand for abandonment of the gold standard and the free coinage of silver in the interest of a stable economy was unthinkable. But accelerating the growth of the banking system so that the same gold monetary base could support more liquid cash was acceptable. Also acceptable was public management of the currency in the interest of preventing panics and crises, and meeting the needs of trade was simply good government. And so the Federal Reserve was born.

Nationalizing the railroads was unthinkable—they were private property. But regulating railroad rates via an Interstate Commerce Commission to protect both shippers against exorbitant charges and the widows and orphans who owned railroad stocks and bonds against destructive competition was common sense.

And some of the more egregious monopolies, such as Standard Oil, could be broken up into several huge companies. And of course there should be a Federal Trade Commission to make sure that business that was big was big because it was more efficient and not because it had conspired to monopolize—especially since the legal tools developed could be used against those other would-be monopolists, the labor unions. Upton Sinclair may have lamented that he had not written his *The Jungle* in order to create the consumer protection wing of the FTC and the Food and Drug Administration—that he "had aimed for America's heart and hit its stomach."[9] But both those who wanted to consume and those who wanted to make and sell on a continent-wide scale aggressively welcomed the assurance provided by the Pure Food and Drug Act and welcomed the freedom from particularistic state-level regulation in support of local interests: Slum clearance. Moral uplift of the poor. Prohibition. The replacement of powerful—and corrupt—directly elected mayors by city managers as the heads of urban bureaucracies. The first environmental movement, conservationism, that created the system of national parks. Regulation of labor, of hours and working conditions—at least for those who, as women and children, could not be expected to be fully self-reliant and who had a just claim on the government to fulfill its role as *pater patriae*. Steps toward social insurance in the form of unemployment compensation, retirement and disability for the exceptionally dangerous jobs of railway workers, and the vast expansion in 1890 of pensions to Northern Civil War soldiers. An income tax, struck down by Republican judges, was finally passed by a constitutional amendment in 1916 with a top rate of 7 percent on incomes of over $500,000 (about $10 million in today's dollars). And more.

Last, in the mid-1920s, came immigration restrictions: the belief that there was something special about the Anglo-Saxon—or at least the northwestern European—population stock that should not be further diluted. This was a big shift: a change from the definition of an American as someone willing to move thousands of miles and cross oceans to seek a better life to someone who looked a lot like the population already here in 1924. This, too, was part of the Progressive movement.

However, three pieces of the Progressive agenda were a bridge too far for the United States between 1890–1925:

- Incorporation into the economic framework of labor unions as a legitimate interest and of collective bargaining as a legitimate mode of interaction

- Tight regulation of high finance

- Social insurance—the full "safety net" as we understand it today

Franklin Roosevelt's New Deal

The redesign led by the New Deal—or rather, in this sole and singular case, the right word is *imposed*—was unlike those that came earlier (with the important exception of the Progressives' course correction)—or later—in that it did not primarily aim to open an important new economic space and do what was needed to get entrepreneurs into it. Instead, it was about emergency treatment for a devastated economy, an America whose vital signs were all terrible. The good doctor, to use the kind of homey terminology Roosevelt loved and the nation adored, had no clear diagnosis and no miracle cures like penicillin. The patient had tried walking it off and sweating it out—what we now call *austerity* (now being tried in Europe). It was shrilly and famously voiced, by Andrew Mellon, Hoover's Secretary of the Treasury:

> . . . liquidate labor, liquidate stocks, liquidate farmers, liquidate real estate . . . purge the rottenness out of the system. People will work harder and live a more moral life. Values will be adjusted and enterprising people will pick up from the less competent people . . .

That hadn't worked.

Now something had to be done and done immediately: provide life support, repair trauma, cauterize wounds, stanch bleedings—do something; do it urgently; see if it helps. But radical actions were likely to produce grotesque results.

By March 1933, when Roosevelt took office, about one-third of non-farm workers were unemployed. About half the home mortgages in America were in default. The stock market had lost about four-fifths of its 1929 value. Farm prices had collapsed, and farmers could not pay their loans. Home building had completely stopped, down about 95 percent from 1928 rates. Automobile production was down to about one fourth of its pre-Depression volume; steel too. The banks were defaulting on their depositors; thousands of them had failed and there was a run on the survivors. The people were hurting and lost; anything might happen. The rich and powerful were scared, the powerless too.

On March 4, 1933, tens of millions of Americans listened to FDR's inaugural address on their radios. They heard a strong, confidant voice that did not promise that "prosperity was just around the corner" but that instead acknowledged their fears.[10] He offered no comprehensive diagnosis, no cure-all, but he promised to immediately take pragmatic, concrete actions to help, to relieve the suffering, to do something.

> This Nation asks for action, and action now . . .
> Our greatest primary task is to put people to work.
> This is no unsolvable problem if we face it wisely
> and courageously. It can be accomplished in part by
> direct recruiting by the government itself, treating
> the task as we would treat the emergency of a war,
> but at the same time, through this employment,
> accomplishing greatly needed projects to stimulate
> and reorganize the use of our natural resources . . .
>
> In our progress towards a resumption of work
> we require two safeguards against a return of the
> evils of the old order; there must be a strict super-
> vision of all banking and credits and investments;
> there must be an end to speculation with other
> people's money, and there must be provision for
> an adequate but sound currency . . . These are the
> lines of attack . . .[11]

Never before—and never since—has America had such active, indeed, hyperactive, government. The whirlwind of actions began immediately. Congress was summoned into a special session the next day.

The run on the banks was the most urgent problem. At 1 a.m. on Monday, March 6, Roosevelt closed the banks, richly declaring a "bank holiday." Five days later, a banking bill had been drafted and sent to Congress; eight hours later, it passed and was signed by the president. When the banks reopened on the next Monday, the run had ceased.

And the government did not take over the banks; it saved them.

Housing was next. As noted half of all home mortgages were in default and home building had stopped completely—the source of one-third of total unemployment. As with banking, rescue drew on plans drawn up, but never seriously implemented by the Hoover administration, mostly because of ideological reluctance. Home mortgage rescue had been passed under Hoover in 1932, but the new Federal Home Loan Bank had done nothing. Of the forty thousand applications received, only four (4) were approved in the final six months of the Hoover Administration. Roosevelt's version, the Homeowner's Loan Corporation, passed in the summer of 1933, helped to finance over one million mortgages in two years.[12]

By late May, a securities and banking regulation system was in place; a year later, the Securities and Exchange Commission was established, with Joseph P. Kennedy, a famous speculator as well as, later, a yet more famous *paterfamilias*, as chair. The wily insider proved effective. Choosing to save the failing and discredited banks rather than nationalizing them demonstrated that the New Deal at its very outset was not an ideological, let alone radical, movement, but rather a perfervid emergency effort guided by a radical dose of pragmatism—try it, see if it works. Its core approach could be called *pragmatic experimentalism*: try one thing and then another; what didn't work was dropped; what worked was quickly expanded. And they didn't try one thing after another; they tried many, many things at the same time. The New Deal was ubiquitous. It was active in most every part of the economy, or so it seemed. It was also fast: big new initiatives and projects were undertaken in a flash, laws and regulations were set out, agencies established, and work begun at breathtaking speed and at scale. This was active government in the extreme.

A Civilian Conservation Corps (CCC) was established by the end of the first month to provide jobs for unemployed young men; by summer, it had enrolled 250,000. Ultimately, three million passed through it. It took them off the streets into army-type camps to work on reforestation, marsh draining, and dam building and provided them with a small wage to send home to their families; it reclaimed both the land and the boys. When an "army" of unemployed and rather desperate war veterans descended on Roosevelt's Washington, their reception provided a stark contrast with what happened to a similar "bonus army"; Hoover had unleashed troops under the command of Douglas MacArthur, who thought it appropriate to greet then with tanks, burned their tents, and violently dispersed the old vets and their wives. Roosevelt ordered decent shelter and food, and sent Eleanor to greet them. He also offered to waive the age requirements for the CCC, and many promptly enrolled. The contrast once again showed the nation that its new government cared about them. Nothing could be more valuable in those troubled times.

The initiatives kept coming: The Federal Emergency Relief Administration distributed about $3 billion in its roughly two years of life (total federal spending was $8 billion in 1929). The repeal of Prohibition, certainly among its most popular actions. Agricultural policies aiming at bolstering farm prices and protecting farm mortgages. The massively funded Public Works Administration (PWA), which put unemployed Americans to work building such major projects as the Triboro Bridge and the Grand Coulee Dam, and later the Works Progress Administration (WPA), which at its peak provided work to three million unemployed Americans, mostly in construction but also writers, actors, and artists (the leading lights of what is now called abstract expressionism—including Mark Rothko and Jackson Pollock—as well as such decidedly non-abstract artists as Grant Wood). By 1936, in the West, the five biggest structures in the world, except perhaps for the Great Wall of China—the Boulder Dam (renamed Hoover) on the Colorado; the Grand Coulee and Bonneville dams on the Columbia; the Shasta Dam on the Sacramento, and the Fort Peck Dam on the upper Missouri—had been completed, opening up vast new areas for development. In the East, the Tennessee Valley Authority's full river basin program was created with the avowed purpose of developing a backward region.

Roosevelt took the dollar off the gold standard and then devalued it, and enacted the entire structure of banking and finance regulations that remained in place until the last year of the twentieth century. The financial regulatory regulation was capped by the Glass-Steagall Act (1933), which separated commercial from investment banking, ringed fenced deposits, and insured them.

Until the New Deal, peacetime America was small government America. In 1931, federal government spending was 3.5 percent of GDP, and about half of federal employees were at the Post Office; the New Deal soon doubled that spending and then some—to put legions of unemployed Americans on its various new payrolls, but it did so reluctantly, not boldly and self-confidently. It was pragmatic expediency.

There was no proto-Keynesianism here. The spending went to emergency measures; it was not conceived as the center of a macroeconomic strategy. The dominant ideology intoned from a scaffolding of hoary theory—do nothing, or very little, and let market forces sort it all out and eventually establish a new, long-term equilibrium—had already proven not to work. But its hold was such that Roosevelt was chary about going too far from its strictures: respect private property; don't print money; balance the budget. Roosevelt even proposed, in his first week, to cut government salaries and cut veterans' pensions by 15 percent to help balance what he called the regular, as distinct from the emergency, budget and found himself with a hellish congressional battle. Alas, Roosevelt was not a Keynesian before Keynes (or even at the very publication of Keynes): he proudly cut the deficit in 1937, just after the economy had picked up smartly. The economy promptly tanked. But he was still a pragmatist: the deficit was restored.

Nowhere in Roosevelt's first inaugural address or in the flurry of the first hundred days are the planks of what we today see as the core of New Deal liberalism. Social Security? The construction of the pro-union NLRB labor-relations framework? Deficit spending and active fiscal and monetary policy management? Big government? None of these are there. The only major plank of New Deal liberalism as a set of policies present in Roosevelt's inaugural address and his first round of actions is financial regulation.

The New Deal was the only redesign that did not focus on opening a new economic space for growth and transformation. It focused on emergency repair, on humanitarian measures, on redistribution, on fairness, and on the control of finance. A great many elements to promote growth were tried in the New Deal, from the experiment in industry-level corporatism that was the National Recovery Administration to the Thurman Arnold–driven antitrust competition policy of the Public Utility Holding Companies Act. But of the major pieces aimed at growth, only two survived: the tight regulation of finance via the separation of commercial from investment banking, and the government's commitment to the role of stabilizing economy-wide spending. The other pieces fell away as Roosevelt, the ultimate pragmatist, followed a strategy of reinforcing successes and consigning failures to the memory hole. The other major pieces of the New Deal that survived—farm price supports and farm subsidies, Social Security, welfare proper, labor unions, and the rest of the safety net—were aimed at re-slicing the pie, not growing it. But that, pragmatically, was what the times demanded of FDR. We have here a paradox.

Although the New Deal was not itself ideological but rather the ultimate in pragmatic policy experimentation, it became the definition of the ideology that was post–World War II American liberalism. It became the model of what government could do and should do.

Chapter 3

The Long Age of Eisenhower

President Dwight David Eisenhower's vision was a full-blown consensus: it was shared by automakers, oil companies, and appliance makers; by builders and bankers; and by vast legions of regular Americans—marching bands and booster squads and outpouring fans—gathered around him on the fifty-yard line of American politics and society. The vision was of an imminent future that was not so much a break with the recognizable past as a projection and huge extension of several of the most attractive aspects of where Franklin D. Roosevelt and Harry S. Truman had led America.

Think of it as a triptych—three big panels, each clear and vibrant, each easy to grasp and appreciate. You would get what you saw: There were no questions of theory or ideology to wrestle with.[1] There were no abstract or hidden processes to unleash.

- In the center, the American Dream: a house surrounded by a green lawn; inside, a big, overstuffed refrigerator, a washing machine, and a television. Kids too, with braces. And of course, in the driveway, a big, sleek car—and at the end of the driveway, a curving lane leading to a broad, smooth highway. Above this picture, the legend proclaimed *For the American Family—You.*

- The right panel of the triptych offered a bold display of military might, titled *Protect The Dream.* Here were nuclear submarines, fighter jets, atomic bombs, rockets, and huge networks of research laboratories inventing away to keep America safe by keeping it technologically far ahead in the second half of the twentieth century, when oceans were no longer sufficient for protection.

- And on the left panel, we see the civilian fruits of government spending (mostly by the military) on science and technology—*The Endless Frontier.* We see commercial airliners; amazing machine tools to sculpt airplane wings and other breakthrough marvels; electricity from nuclear reactors that would be too cheap to meter; radar ranges to zap-cook a meal in an instant; and medicines and vaccines—after all, penicillin was still new and the memory of its miracle powers powerful, and Jonas Salk along with Einstein were the universally hailed scientific geniuses. There were to be all kinds of new, impossible-to-understand but thrilling-to-imagine wonders like Dick Tracy telephone-watches and giant computers to do whatever it would be that computers were to do. It was easy, even uplifting to accept.

The vision seemed to have no downside, and though exciting and new, all of it was familiar. There were no radical departures, no ruptures, no risks, no losers on the face of it—perhaps just a few who might not get on board and benefit.

Everything was already out there. Developed technologies: air-conditioners (which enabled the military budget–driven growth of the Sun Belt); cars with automatic transmissions and radios, power steering, and their own air-conditioners; television, freezers, dishwashers, clothes washers, dryers, and commercial aviation with jets just on the runway. Accepted models and forms: balloon-frame, tract-built, affordable suburban houses and limited-access highways.

Now all, or at least most, American families were going to get them. And the institutions, structures, and policies that would make it happen, like the fully developed technologies and model suburbs, were also already in place: big corporations, big unions, and a big, active government overseeing and supporting private enterprise in ways that had become familiar—mortgage financing for single-family homes; road building; defense spending and its spin-offs; tight and steady regulation of finance; and government oversight of big business and big unions. It was all in place by the time Ike came to office and authoritatively assured its continuation and its massive, smooth, and responsible expansion. Government would continue to do what was needed to enable the full-blown reshaping of the economy, and the shape was already chosen.

Back then, there were some in the Democratic party on the left who wanted a more comprehensive social democracy than FDR or Truman were offering (or that Kennedy or even Johnson would offer); there were many in the Southern wing of the Democratic Party who wanted to dismantle big government, especially what didn't directly subsidize their states. And there were many in the Republican Party—though not quite as many as now—who wanted to dismantle the structures of big government and its regulatory control over the economy—undo the New Deal—and return to something resembling the 1920s. But then, unlike now, they were smartly defeated by Ike and the moderate, middle-class-focused, corporate Republicans—the establishment. Under a Republican banner, Ike legitimized big government with its New Deal structures and institutions.

As Eisenhower wrote to his brother Edgar in 1954:

> This country is following a dangerous trend when it permits too great a degree of centralization . . . I oppose this . . . But to attain any success it is quite clear that the Federal government cannot avoid or escape responsibilities which the mass of the people firmly believe should be undertaken by it . . . If a rule of reason is not applied in this effort, we will lose everything . . . Should any political party attempt to abolish social security, unemployment insurance, and eliminate labor laws and farm programs, you would not hear of that party again in our political history. There is a tiny splinter group, of course, that believes you can do these things. Among them are

H. L. Hunt (you possibly know his background), a few other Texas oil millionaires, and an occasional politician or businessman from other areas. Their number is negligible and they are stupid . . .[2]

Under a Republican banner, Ike ended rather than won the Korean War. He then prevented the nation from plunging into scapegoating, recrimination, divisiveness and a politics even more virulent and worse than the McCarthyism he inherited. This by-and-large comfortable legitimization of the New Deal flowed like a broad river through the eight years of Eisenhower's presidency, then the eight years of New Deal Democrats Kennedy and Johnson, then eight years of Republicans Nixon and Ford. It weakened in the four years of Democrat Carter. It dried up in the desert when the Reagan Revolution dammed it and set out to delegitimize the idea—though not the budget—of New Deal big and active government. The Reagan administration began the work of dismantling its regulatory structures. But remember that the president who stated flatly in his State of the Union address that "the era of Big Government is over" was not Ronald Reagan but Bill Clinton.

In Eisenhower's America, government knew how to spend: it spent big-time, and taxed big-time too. It was big government and then some. Federal spending under Eisenhower was 18 percent of GDP—twice what it had been in peacetime even at the height of FDR's New Deal. And state and local government spending raised total government spending to over 30 percent. As noted in chapter 2, in pre–New Deal

1931, federal spending was 3.5 percent of GDP, and a half of all federal employees were in the Post Office. Federal government direct employment was 5,354,000 in 1962. And that was in a nation of some 180 million people. In 2010, there were 4,443,000 government employees and the population was over 300 million. It was definitely big government. This very large flow of government cash immune to the vagaries of the business cycle, business confidence, or other animal spirits enabled and provided for vigorous and profitable private initiative. And high taxes, not high borrowings, paid for big government: federal deficits averaged less than 1 percent of GDP from 1950 to 1970.[3]

Ike's was a conservative approach, preserving and expanding existing institutions and roles that not many years earlier had been thought radical, and building on them in a way that was socially unthreatening and very business friendly. That is quite different from a radical Right approach, nowadays confusingly called Conservative, which aims at dismantling the structures of the economy to produce rather radical, often romantically envisioned, change.

Ike's mainstream Republican conservatives—and Nixon's— also conserved the new American income distribution. In the postwar generation, productivity grew at about a real 2 percent per year, and so did median incomes (roughly doubling during a working life). So too did the incomes of the top 10 percent.[4] As conservatives, these presidents didn't seek to create a new income distribution as both the New Deal and the "Reagan Revolution" and its successors set out to do and succeeded in doing, albeit in different directions.

It seems as though there were no major reshufflings of rank. There was no a surge in individual mobility. Thus, the children of the top 5 percent or 10 percent were likely twenty years later to be in that same 5 or 10 percent. What did change, however, was general prosperity: the steady rise of the median and even the next fifth earners into something they regarded as a better, middle-class life. The cars, houses, appliances, and nice schools that had been reserved for the top 10 percent in 1929 became the property of, or at least within sight of, the majority by 1970. This, in its own steady way, was both untroubling and revolutionary. It was certainly something quite unforeseen in the miserable 1930s. It was hugely welcome.

Many factors contributed to this sustained "fairness," or equality in gain, among which a prominent position must be granted to highly progressive income tax rates that climbed steeply, bracket after bracket, up to a confiscatory 91 percent. Big unions defended the wage share. There was also a culture of appropriate shares: then CEO pay, the top of the heap, was about thirty times that of the average company worker (now it is about three hundred times as much, and it would be difficult indeed, to make a case that today's CEOs perform in any way better).[5] Under the New Deal/Eisenhower regime of regulation, finance became something of a utility: incomes in the finance sector were in line with incomes in manufacturing or insurance or other broad sectors. Bankers had good but quiet lives, protected against competition on price by regulations on what interest rates they could pay, and as a result insulated from the need to search for yield and focused on competing via offering convenience and toasters. It was only with the accelerating deregulation of finance that their incomes soared away from other sectors. And under the long period from Truman to Reagan, finance seemed to work just fine: capital flowed, business prospered, houses were built. And there were no financial crises.

Suburbanization

Federal government efforts to promote home building and home ownership by making mortgage finance on longer terms available to more people with worse credit actually began under Herbert Hoover. Home building had fallen by 95 percent between 1928 and 1932. Perhaps a third of unemployment was due to the complete destruction of construction. By early 1933 close to one half of all homes in the United States were technically in default.[6] In August 1932, Herbert Hoover signed the Federal Home Loan Bank Act to provide government credit for mortgages on houses. It set out what was to become the American approach to government promotion and assistance for housing. Instead of direct government provision of housing (which became the norm in Europe), there would be substantial government support for the financing of the private development and ownership of houses. Hoover, however, did not have his heart in it. In the program's six months, over forty thousand applications for mortgages were received, but only three (three) were approved.[7] It took the New Deal to make federal policy for home building and ownership real enough, big enough and fast enough to matter. The change was dramatic. Roosevelt took office in March 1933. His Homeowners Loan Corporation (HOLC; founded in June 1933) helped to finance over one million mortgages between August 1933 and August 1935. Moreover, it set in place what became the enduring mechanisms of US mortgage financing: long-term fixed rates, low down payment, amortization—and backstopped by the government guarantee necessary to persuade banks that it was good business to lend at a fixed rate for thirty years to borrowers who always had the option to pay off at any instant. In the 1920s, by contrast, first mortgages were typically for about half of the appraised value. They ran for five or ten years with a balloon payment at the end, which could be refinanced—if times were good and so was the borrower's credit.[8] HOLC was soon followed by the Federal Housing Administration (FHA), created in June 1934, which became the institutional centerpiece of American housing policy for the rest of the century. Its mission was to promote private home building and home ownership without direct federal expenditure. The FHA did not finance mortgages out of the federal till; it insured privately written mortgages for as long as thirty years (for fixed-rate mortgages) with down payments of under 10 percent. And interest payments and real estate taxes were tax-deductible: the higher your income and the bigger your house, the larger your tax subsidy in post–World War II America, in which the income tax was paid not just by the rich but by the middle class as well.

In 1944, with the end of the war in sight, the government was worried about how sixteen million returning GIs would find jobs. It passed the GI Bill, providing in place of a traditional veteran's bonus a generous program of support for GIs wishing to go to college, plus a major mortgage assistance program with the valuable extra kicker of a possibly zero down payment. FHA insurance, the guarantor of the American Dream, and with it the quasi-totality of government housing policy, was focused intensely on freestanding single-family houses. The government insured seven single-family units for each apartment, and built only one public housing apartment for every thirty-three private dwelling units.[9]

Developments of single-family houses on lots of even one-fifth or one-tenth of an acre meant automobiles. Geometry dictated. Given the scale and rapidity of their growth, the model of the older streetcar suburbs or commuter train villages would not work. Limited-access highways as stupendous, omnipresent circulatory systems were the necessary enablers. This was the other arm—the big-budget part—of the government's ambitious program to reshape the economy, the society, and the landscape. The National Defense Highway Act (1956) was the biggest public works program between the Egyptian pyramids and the great Chinese urbanization at the turn of the twenty-first century. It called for forty-one thousand miles of high-speed highways, with the federal government paying 90 percent of the costs. They were physically engineered for limited external access and politically engineered for zero external access to their funding source: the gasoline tax. Nothing else could tap the Highway Trust Fund, a rare departure for a major tax source. Transportation money was even more sharply skewed to the suburbs and away from the needs of the cities than FHA insurance: only about 1 percent of federal transportation funding went to mass transit. And two-thirds of the highway lane miles were built within the boundaries of metropolitan areas: the interstate highway system should have been named the suburban highway system. Thus America became a suburban nation by design and with broad enthusiasm. About 80 percent of the nation's growth in the postwar generation was in the suburbs (three-quarters of its largest cities lost population).[10]

In the great migration to the suburbs, all but the poorest ranks of American families found their place and felt it to be the same place: middle-class America. Social scientists had difficulty understanding how and why a hefty majority of Americans persisted in saying that they were middle-class. Americans happily marched, or rather drove, out to take possession of their new suburban homes. Admittedly, some houses were bigger and better than others; they had bigger lawns and bigger rooms and, crucially, they were surrounded by similar bigger houses. The progression of status and wealth signaled by the differentiation of suburbs was finely calibrated and well understood. There was no suspicious Continental egalitarianism or leveling. Suburban development was an extreme form of segregation by class and, of course, by race. But the hierarchy of status and wealth did not delineate separate worlds. There were no "two nations." There was one nation—middle-class America—with some having more and better of the same thing.

Indeed, there was a new kind of built-in democratization, or homogenization, in the consumption patterns of what we are calling the Long Age of Ike. The suburban form itself—the house and lawn, the car, and the goods pouring out of triumphant mass production—was democratic in its fundamental sameness, differentiated by degree, not kind. And it was reinforced by the equal proportional rates at which steady growth in incomes was distributed. The rich man's television often had a mahogany cabinet and two or even four inches in screen size over the less expensive models, and all were growing bigger and better with the regular introduction of new models. But they all received the same programs from the dominant three national networks and they all were used a lot. They all got their news from those stations—a rather important development—as well as their shared entertainment. For breakfast, they all had—along with the same milk, bread, and butter—a large variety of cereal in boxes, all coming from the same three or four companies. They all washed their hands and faces with Lux or Palmolive or Ivory, and brushed their teeth with toothpaste from the same three companies (Procter & Gamble, Unilever, and Colgate-Palmolive). Their refrigerators and washers and dryers were differentiated in only the small details. By and large, everyone also saw the same movies and heard the same music (though increasingly separated by generations as the 1950s rolled on). Overwhelmingly, they sent their kids to the public school, a powerful drive for neighborhood separation and homogenization. And of course, the rich man's Cadillac had many features to signal that it was better and certainly more expensive than the plainer man's Chevrolet, but they shared about 85 percent of the same parts.[11]

Everyone accepted the signaling of expensiveness and ranking in cars, houses, and neighborhoods and the obligation to try to climb a bit. But everyone also accepted that these were degrees, not differences in kind: out in the suburbs, they all were, they strongly felt, in middle-class America. Life echoed the closing line in Ernst Troeltsch's masterful study, *The Social Teaching of the Christian Churches*, "In paradise, Beatrice tells her poet, it doesn't matter if there are differing degrees of celestial bliss, because all is joy."

At least for white America. For in America's new suburbia, everyone was white.

Race

By 1960, Long Island's Levittown had eighty-two thousand residents—and they were all white.[12] Many factors contributed to the strict segregation by class, or at least income, and especially by race, that characterized—perhaps even defined—the new suburban America.

America was a profoundly racist society, by history, by law and custom, and by inclination. But on the list of contributing factors was deliberate, government-enforced intention at every level, local to federal. Government—as policy maker and as judiciary—imposed and enforced racial segregation. FHA was not only the main federal government player in suburban development, but principal promoter of suburban racial segregation. FHA insurance was available only after a property had been rigorously and professionally appraised—only correct practice for what quickly became the world's biggest property insurer. The elaborate guidelines it developed for professional appraisal quickly became the professional template. The FHA appraisal forms gave points for social as well as physical conditions in determining the value of the property, and racial segregation figured prominently in this government protocol. As Michael Carliner, economist at the National Association of Homebuilders, wrote, "The FHA underwriting standard included a mandate that the neighborhood be 'homogeneous' (segregated), with that homogeneity preferably assured through racist restrictive covenants, for which the FHA helpfully supplied forms."[13]

The intense concentration of federal housing and transportation programs on the racially restricted suburbs—one percent of the massive transportation monies went to mass transit and 85 percent of FHA mortgage insurance went to the suburbs—powerfully propelled white families out of the cities and into the suburbs. These policies also generated blowback or, in this case, "left-back." Moving white America out of the city left in its wake a self-disorganizing urban pathology. As more and more white families moved out, more and more white families felt that they had to move out. City schools were being stripped of their white, middle-class students and left with what was broadly perceived as the detritus: African Americans and ever-lower-class white children, as well as shrinking tax bases.

White flight became a major driver of suburban growth and urban decay. African Americans were trapped behind, in what came to be called the *inner city*. Jobs too relocated to the suburbs, not just retail in the new shopping centers, but almost every type of enterprise. Highway junctions, rather than center city, became the preferred location for regional distribution; manufacturing could build more efficient, single-level plants (and trucks could get in and out faster); and office jobs were attracted to the white-collar workforce now in the suburbs— and by proximity to the boss's new home. The small amount of public housing (3 percent of total starts) was concentrated in the inner cities, and rules for eligibility for public housing increasingly made them depositories of the most disadvantaged and dysfunctional families. The *projects*, as they came to be called, were threatening islands of poverty and crime— zones to be avoided. Also remaining behind were those non– African Americans who couldn't move out, or chose not to: singles; those without kids; the poorer; and the older, including members of the extended families of the new suburbanites who used to live right by Mama and Aunt Peggy and Aunt Maria, still hanging on in the old neighborhoods.

The separation of the proximate extended family contributed to the great American loneliness and also to the rising monetary cost of doing all those little and not-so-little daily tasks that formerly would be taken care of by nearby family members, especially child and elder care. And, of course, building of a nation of poorly insulated, single-family homes on large lots utterly dependent on automobile use created a nation locked into much higher energy use than other countries that became comparably rich—twice as high as even Germany, which is proportionally much more industrial. The crisis of inner cities hit America rather quickly; the crisis of oil dependency came later; the crisis of burning carbon profligately is only now being reluctantly, catastrophically, belatedly understood. And those seventy-some-odd million houses on large lots will not be replaced anytime soon.

Protecting the Dream

The right-hand panel is very big and quite exciting—high-tech too. Press a button and you are on the flight deck of a nuclear-powered aircraft carrier with jets taking off; press another button and you are inside a jet fighter, dogfighting, diving, and bombing a column of tanks; press yet another and you see a rocket rise; two presses and it rises not from a land station, but from a submarine. Boys and congressmen and journalists love it.

Defense was very big indeed. Ike and his corporate conservatives conserved not just the New Deal's regulatory and economic structures (especially financial regulation and, to a lesser extent, labor regulation), not just the income distribution (which stayed pretty constant through twenty years of growth), but, after Ike ended the Korean War, a high level of military spending. Military spending did come down from the Korean War's 1954 high of about 14 percent of GDP, but not precipitously as it had done after past wars; instead, it steadied stubbornly at about 10 percent—about two and a half times the amount spent under the Clinton and George W. Bush administrations.[14] This was quite different from what happened after World War II, when military spending as a proportion of GDP hit its super wartime high of 38 percent of GDP in 1944, then plummeted to about 4 percent in 1948.

After that low, the build-up seemed to know no bounds: by 1950, the United States had three hundred nuclear bombs in its arsenal; by 1960, eighteen thousand; by 1970, twenty-six thousand.[15] In 1954, America launched its nuclear-powered submarine program; in 1960, the first nuclear-powered submarine—*Polaris*—able to launch a nuke. Then again, there were the Russians, and the Cold War; it was, in a famous earlier phrase, neither war nor peace.[16] And so was the budget.

It was big government under Ike—and through the Nixon and Kennedy administrations too—especially big military: a permanent war economy, in effect. And it worked. It held the Russians at bay; it kept employment high and productivity growing (at about 2 percent per year); and it distributed that gain squarely to all incomes—not skewed to the top, as for the past twenty-five years, but at the same 2 percent real growth rate to top incomes and to the median income, doubling all of them in twenty-five years. High taxes, not high borrowings, paid for big government; federal deficits averaged less than 1 percent (including some years of small surpluses) from 1950 to 1970.[17] And the vast sums pumped into the economy went round and round. They didn't leak out. Imports accounted for only about 3 percent of GDP throughout the 1950s and 1960s, and exports were a bit higher, resulting in a positive balance of trade.

Beyond its primary principal purpose of standing down the Soviets, military spending served many secondary objectives. It was a principal instrument of the federal government's effort to develop the still backward, rural South, which had began in earnest in the New Deal (the TVA's rural electrification program) and continued through that great trough of fiscal federalism, the Interstate Highway System constructed under the National Interstate and Defense Highways Act. In 1950, the census-defined region of the South had a per capita income of 63 percent of the national average; by 1970 it had increased smartly to 74 percent.[18] Military spending was certainly not the only factor at play here. Air-conditioning had an outsized role; out-migration from the Deep South affected the averages quite substantially, as did the inbound migration of labor-intensive industries such as textiles and apparel from high-wage New England and Mid-Atlantic states. Most of the Far West was a near desert. Little rain fell, and most of its surface water was confined within three mountain-runoff river systems: the Colorado in the Southwest, the Columbia in the Northwest, and the Sacramento–San Joaquin in California. Damming and controlling these great river systems continued all through the New Deal and the long Age of Ike and made possible such great cities as Los Angeles, Las Vegas and Phoenix, as well as California agriculture and the huge population growth of those regions.[19]

Military spending shifted toward the South and the Southwest from the Northeast and Midwest. In part this reflected a shift to airpower, in part the continuation of deliberate regional development policy, and in no small measure from the disproportionate and generally permanent position of Southern senators and congressmen on the key committees that controlled the military budget.

Growth of a leading sector that over time reshapes the economy usually translates into a corresponding reshaping of politics; it generates a new locus of political power with its own self-interested goals—the rise of an apparently permanent war economy is the classic, if not most recent, example. The first focus of such sector growth typically is the preservation and enhancement of its own economic position through political means. In the case of the military, the defense budget is the primary focus. Toward that end, the military would use its budget to secure the political strength needed to support and expand that budget, typically by locating military expenditures first to key and eventually to a broad range of congressional districts, to buy its own support.

Echoing faintly and distantly George Washington's famous farewell address with its warning about "entangling foreign alliances," Eisenhower in his own farewell address (January 17, 1961) warned the nation about the dangers posed by the permanent war economy: "In the councils of government, we must guard against the acquisition of unwarranted influence, whether sought or unsought, by the military-industrial complex. The potential for the disastrous rise of misplaced power exists, and will persist."[20]

The Endless Frontier

A bubbling transparent tube connected *Protecting the Dream* to the third panel of the triptych: *Science and Technology: The Endless Frontier*, a marvelously evocative name and rationale: basic science to technology to both defense and the civil economy.

This display involved a lot of imagineering because of what it promised—science and technology that would bring forth entirely new things. New things are inherently less easy to visualize and appreciate, or even understand, than the suburban houses, cars, and washing machines depicted in the first panel or the atomic bombs, jet fighters, aircraft carriers, and rockets in the second. But the first items that appeared along something of a time line demanded little imagination: nuclear-generated electricity that would be too cheap to meter; jet airliners to whisk Americans across the continent and across the ocean; radar ovens to zap dinner; and—why not?— wristwatch telephones, just like in the comics. There were also funny kinds of screens—half-radar, half-television, it seemed—with flashing dots and numbers, surrounded by flashing vacuum tubes and lots of men in white lab coats. The whole thing was labeled "computers" and was marked by high promise in the rapidly approaching future. Hard to comprehend, but still exciting. And, of course, right up front with the atomic bomb were the polio vaccine and penicillin—the three great, universally understood instances of the transformative power of science.

Mission focus was real; it was not just a smokescreen for industrial policy. The military's support of R&D stayed mission-focused. But it was the Pentagon that operationalized the definition of mission and what that mission required for success. When the Navy thought that nuclear propulsion would permit a submarine equipped with nuclear-tipped missiles to cruise deep under water and thereby arm the Navy with a decisive weapon and also provide America with an unstoppable second-strike potential, it set about developing one. When the Air Force thought it should develop jet tankers to refuel combat planes midair, it went ahead and did it. Or when it thought that newly invented (at Bell Labs) transistors could replace all those big, hot, and forever failing vacuum tubes in the tight cabin of a jet fighter—as well as upgrade all kinds of other technology systems—it sponsored the development of the transistor and then semiconductor technology in a big way. Or when it thought that it should try to create a very long line of radar stations to provide early warnings of Soviet attacks, even though to function it would require truly huge leaps in computer and communications technology, it did so, at impressive cost—and with impressive results, at least in the realm of advancing computer capability. And finally, because the military budget was such a vast mansion, with so many rooms (many containing black rooms, some of which contained smaller black rooms), it could with ease start funding research and development—though not massive acquisition programs—for just about whatever it felt to be interesting to its purposes.

Military planners were not blind to the great value these technologies might hold for the civilian economy, though like everybody else, they had no idea of just how huge some of them would become. So where they felt it to be appropriate, they would organize transfers out to the civilian economy. Very soon they even had a word for the process: spin-off.

The result was a big-budget, dual-use success. Military technological superiority was maintained (and accelerated after the embarrassing fright of *Sputnik*), and America also got a far-sighted, powerful, and hugely successful industrial policy that reshaped the economy toward what we now call digital and *advanced technology* and its ever more pervasive and transformative uses. But it was spin-off, a decidedly secondary objective, not an effort to primarily target or directly subsidize the civilian economy. Despite the very positive economic experience of big, active government during the New Deal and World War II, the United States was not going to create a statist economy (outside the important parenthesis of defense). Rather, we were going to lead our allies and the undecided nations of the rest of the world (at least that very large part of the world outside the clutches of anti-market, anti-democratic, totalitarian Soviet communism), like a good parent—ever gently but decidedly—to appreciate and adopt a liberal democratic, open-market-based world economy rooted in private enterprise values and institutions. And so we did; in Europe, Japan, and later and slower, in Korea and Taiwan, and we did so with considerable pragmatism, at least as far as economic structures and policies were concerned. US policy makers believed that government should do only what only government can do—and clear the way for private business. But they were not terribly insistent on our European allies hurrying toward that goal, nor overly concerned about even defining demarcations between what was the rightful economic role of government and what wasn't.

State-owned enterprises dominating the key sectors of the economy? Fine. France's huge, and rather high-performance, state-owned sectors—banking, electricity, energy, aircraft, airlines, cigarettes, railways, broadcasting, telecommunications, and many others—were not privatized until almost fifty years after the war, and then not because of direct pressure by US policy makers (it had been a long time since the US could exert such direct pressure), but by the new structures and rules of the EU; Spain and Italy had something similar. And when capital was extremely scarce in France in the days of the Marshall Plan, government planning to allocate that scarce capital among industries seemed like a good idea. So did doing effectively the same thing through a few dominant banks that interlocked with the major companies in West Germany.

Price controls? Currency controls? Of course—quite necessary, given the conditions, if not exactly blessed. And speedy dismantlement of these temporary expedients was not demanded. Formal capital controls stayed in place in Japan until 1980, and less formal ones a lot longer; France, Finland, and Sweden, in the words of an OECD report, "started liberalizing the hard core of the capital control regime" in the mid-1980s and didn't complete the job until about five years later.[21]

The Cold War dominated American policy and politics.

It was framed less as a geopolitical standoff than as an ideological struggle—liberal democratic, market capitalism versus totalitarian, Communist statism—and therefore richly generative of ideological flag-waving and hysteria, both of which ran amok in the United States for an ugly while. But given these conditions, American policy for the economy—its own and those of its allies—was remarkably free of ideology; it was, all in all, quite pragmatic in its means and concrete in its objectives. Even when America had inordinate influence, just after the Marshall Plan and extending right through the 1950s, we supported the dominant statist economic institutions and policies of most of our European allies and rather encouraged the resurrection of the *zaibatsu*—Japanese industrial and financial business consortia, later rechristened *keiretsu*—after we had so vigorously, as the occupying power, dismantled them.

US policy makers, especially the military planners, understood that basic research and early development—the first critical steps toward the "endless frontier" and toward permanent military technological superiority—could not be left to private enterprises, though they could be contracted to them.

Basic research was far too costly, far too risky, and worst of all, just too uncertain to be undertaken at the contemplated scale by private firms dependent on capital markets. There were a few big exceptions. The most important by far, in ways impossible to exaggerate, was Bell Laboratories, the science and invention powerhouse of the economy. Bell Labs was the research arm of AT&T, the regulated telecom monopoly, and also a substantial defense contractor. Legally a private firm, Bell Labs was in reality nothing of the sort. It could do basic research without very much bottom line or financial risk, and had a deep culture of doing just that.[22] It also was a favorite government contractor. IBM too achieved an important research capability, but it was developed later, mostly through military contracts. So where it could, in good conscience, government stepped in, took on the risk, and took the lead. Though non-military government agencies such as the National Science Foundation (NSF) grew to substantial scale, it was overwhelmingly the military (and its close cousins at NASA and the Atomic Energy Commission) that designed, funded, and oversaw R&D and just as important, usually filled the critical role of substantial launch client.

Nuclear Power

Government has always tightly controlled most everything pertaining to nuclear energy. Though the nuclear power generators were built by private companies and the power plants were constructed by private companies for their operators, which were private utilities, the entire industry was invented, developed, and overseen by the government and treated as something special—quite different from airliners and semiconductors, computers and software, let alone steel or engines. As the director of the Lawrence Livermore Laboratory told one of us, "We're not in favor of entrepreneurship in nuclear matters."

As well as more and more nuclear bombs, the American government had been developing nuclear power reactors throughout the late 1940s and early 1950s. A Navy program built on this work to develop reactors to run nuclear-powered submarines and nuclear-powered aircraft carriers, prime mission objectives for Navy planners. Adaptation of these models to generate electricity for the civilian economy created a big industry, with American firms such as Westinghouse, a prime contractor, dominating globally.[23] In the shadow of war's nuclear catastrophe, electricity from nuclear generators was thought to provide a bright spot, a promise of important peaceful uses of atomic energy, and even a plausible offset to the staggering costs of the nuclear programs.

In 1954, Lewis Strauss, chairman of the Atomic Energy Commission, forecast that in our children's time, nuclear energy would be "too cheap to meter."[24] President Eisenhower shared this optimistic view, and took the grand promise—along with offers to establish negotiations toward international controls to lessen the catastrophic threat of nuclear warfare—to the UN General Assembly in his famous "Atoms for Peace" address, in which he offered to provide nuclear power technology not just to America's European allies, but to developing nations, for which it was thought, this technology would be economically transformative.[25] The address was delivered on December 8, 1953—seven months before the Soviets inaugurated the first civilian nuclear power plant. The US technology was turned over to America's electricity utilities and shared with its principal allies via Westinghouse and other contractors. It was widely proliferated as American firms built and licensed the construction of nuclear power stations and trained nuclear engineers, with US government approval and support, in many countries—including, eventually, Iran and Pakistan—thus launching their nuclear trajectories. Nuclear power grew globally.

Then, in the United States at least, growth halted quite suddenly. No new reactors have been constructed in the United States since 1979, the year of the Three Mile Island accident, although nuclear plants still account for perhaps a fifth of total US electricity generation (very roughly $75 billion) and for nearly half in France, the nuclear energy champ. The promise of atoms for peace has not yet been realized. Nuclear reactors did not become a way to lift impoverished countries toward prosperity and peace. Outside the Navy, they have played no role in transportation. They did not revolutionize medicine. And no experience with nuclear power has proved to be too cheap to meter. Some have proved too costly to count. Admittedly, the industry that was spun off from military R&D was huge; the ironies, however were, arguably, huger still. And the game is not yet over.

Commercial Jetliners

Commercial jetliners too were spun out of the military's research, development, and procurement programs and almost instantly became a giant American industry rich in value added, generating whole new areas of economic activity and glamorously powerful as a symbol of American technical/industrial leadership for peoples of all nations, and also for the most important audience right at home. Boeing, with some luck and agility, landed the contract for the KC-135 Stratotanker, designed to refuel jet fighters and bombers in midair. The Pentagon financed its costly development and bought very substantial quantities over a long period of time. That sustained support extended to the development of highly specialized machine tools. The aircraft was powered by jet engines, also developed—at whopping costs and risks—under Air Force contracts that even covered developments in metallurgy needed to make those engines. The Boeing 707 commercial jetliner came down the same assembly line as the KC-135 and could be reasonably, if lightheartedly, thought of as the KC-135 with windows. Both were very slight adaptations of their Boeing 367-80 prototype.[26] The 707 quickly achieved dominance. From 0 percent of the US commercial aircraft market in 1958, Boeing hit 30 percent in 1959 and 92 percent in 1964, and dominated globally.[27] Boeing held its unchallenged dominance until the end of the 1980s, when Airbus—the prime symbol of Europe uniting to achieve the scale and technological capacity necessary for its future and the recipient of years and years of massive subsidies—rose to challenge that dominance, and kept rising to achieve parity in a duopoly that nervously awaits a massively subsidized Chinese competitor.

Microwave Ovens

And of course, there was the microwave oven, which always pops up in lists of spin-off successes. Though economically of rather marginal, even trivial importance compared with commercial jets, nuclear power, or the whole kit and caboodle of computing and advanced telecommunications, the microwave oven—called at the time a *radar range*—came right out of defense programs. It was born at Raytheon, a major defense contractor, especially in radar. Legend has it that a Raytheon engineer placed a bag of popcorn outside a wave guard driven by a magnetron from a military radar set and noticed that the kernels began to pop. Raytheon commercialized the first restaurant oven in 1947 and, moving at the speed of a major defense contractor, marketed the first one for home use in 1965. Technology historian John Alic and his colleagues cite the microwave as the epitome of pure spin-off, as a "free, non-targeted alternative to technology policy . . . no direct government effort is needed to ensure its success."[28] (And Raytheon eventually lost the market to Asian competitors.)

Launching the Digital Age

The truly transformative, or foundational, success was information technology. The pervasive new digital environment in which we now work and live was launched by the policies of the long Eisenhower consensus—even though they are only having their full visible effect today. Just about all of it came spinning out of federal research, development, and procurement programs, overwhelmingly from the military and, a bit later, from NASA.

The Pentagon, NASA, the Department of Energy's National Labs, and the NSF, especially through Bell Labs, drove and supported the R&D that yielded the key inventions and launched initial applications that led to their exponential growth. The inventions were fundamental, revolutionary building blocks—transistors and semiconductors, the laser, fiber optics, computers and the software to run them in real time, the internet, artificial intelligence, and satellite technology, not to mention the creation and funding of computer science departments at universities to develop the skilled personnel needed to advance them all. With few exceptions, the inventions that opened up whole new industries and transformed most others did not come from kids in Silicon Valley garages or even, as was more generally the case until the present moment of companies requiring only very small investments to innovate algorithms and apps, but from somewhat older, more experienced entrepreneur-innovators who spun out of other companies, programs, and universities.[29] They did not invent. They innovated adaptations, applications, and new uses and did so with wonderful inventiveness and imagination, speeding proliferation in a way that Pentagon contractors, or even large mature corporations, never could have matched, and did not. This is just what was supposed to happen: government enables or opens up a new economic space, provides what is needed to launch, and entrepreneurs pour in to fill it and go on to create whole new products and industries and in the process reshape the economy.

It was the high time of spin-off: government, especially the military and the space program, urgently needed what the new technologies promised and were willing and able to invest long-term into high uncertainty. For a critically long time, government was the lead user as well as the smart, patient, and very deep-pocketed, risk-taking investor. And there was an American industrial capacity with the right skills to run with it, equip the military and develop, adapt, and apply the technology to produce new civilian goods: this was the famous "spillover" effect. And it "spilled over" round after round, usually within a small geographic range, and transformed the economy. Entrepreneurs, capital, and skills had to be right here at home for the spin-off model to generate positive economic redesign. Up until the last years of the twentieth century they were, and the model worked marvelously.

The Pentagon drove the development of semiconductor technology and a robust, competitive American semiconductor industry—the young firms that gave Silicon Valley its name: Fairchild, Intel, National Semiconductor, AMD, and their proliferating brethren. In the very early years of this technology, the Pentagon was the market; it bought 95 percent of total production, at high prices.[30] And it was the Pentagon, more than anyone else, that set in motion an ecology of young competitive semiconductor firms, rather than just feeding a few giants.

This was, to say the least, quite unusual for Pentagon procurement; historically, since the days of Eli Whitney, the most valuable asset for a defense contractor has been the right senator's address. But once the Pentagon saw that it was becoming dependent on young, unproven—and quite probably fragile—firms for what was becoming a vital technology, it insisted on "dual sourcing."[31] This forced the diffusion of the technology to producers. And this shaped the market structure of the industry: many fast-moving, new firms, growing at unprecedented rates, but few real monopolies.

Within a few years of breathtaking improvements in semiconductor capability and reliability, the commercial market had grown to vastly exceed the Pentagon's share. And so was born Gordon Moore's extrapolation, later called *Moore's Law*: every eighteen months, semiconductor performance doubled. The next twenty-five years of compounding improvements in semiconductor performance and the development of myriad applications, including desktop computers, laptops, calculators, appliances, automotive systems, machinery—everything—owed nothing to the Pentagon and everything to the competitive entrepreneurial environment.

In the exciting experimental computer era of the 1950s and 1960s, the nascent digital industry needed government support, indeed sponsorship. Between 1966 and 1989, the number of bachelor's degrees in computer science increased from a mere sixty-six to forty-two thousand.[32] This was not because universities or businesses thought the bet worth taking, but because the NSF stepped into the game in an important and sustaining way: it set out to provide universities with computers for general education and scientific applications. As a National Research Council report put it, the NSF essentially decided it "would pay for American campuses to enter the computer age."[33]

The computer age can be said to have begun with ENIAC, the first digital computer developed at the University of Pennsylvania and funded by the Army Research Laboratory (ARL) in 1946. This was the fabled caricature of the early computer: it filled a giant room and was tended by a legion of white-coated assistants running about replacing popping vacuum tubes, pulling levers, pushing buttons, taking notes. Later in 1946 came the next stage: the Navy launched Project Whirlwind, a device intended for a general-purpose flight simulator. By 1949, Whirlwind was eating up about 10 percent of the Navy's research budget without a useful device to show for the effort. In such a situation—vast expenditures, no results, and the likely bureaucratic penalties of declaring failure— the Pentagon reacted as it often does. The failure of Whirlwind to work showed only that it needed to be done again at a much larger scale.

The only way to salvage the program was to expand it by what proved to be orders of magnitude. Whirlwind was folded into SAGE, the Air Force's project for a string of computer-connected radar stations facing the Arctic, to provide early warning of Soviet missiles. The setup called for round-the-clock, real-time computing system coordination. The project was a long-term, big-budget extravaganza; its costs eventually exceeded those of the Manhattan Project.[34] The system as designed and ultimately implemented did not have much of an effect on American security. Satellite technology (*Sputnik* was launched in 1958) made it instantly obsolete.

But it generated scores of innovations—magnetic core memory, digital phone-line transmission, and real-time software. And with these, SAGE lifted computing from a scientific to an economic phenomenon. It provided the basis of America's two-generation-plus unchallengeable domination of that most important of new industries and technologies—a domination that continues today.

Under Pentagon contract, IBM made the SAGE computers, creating key innovations and embodying others; and SAGE made IBM. IBM built fifty-six computers for the project, earning over $500 million (over $4 billion in today's dollars). Out of SAGE came a small legion of experienced computer designers and programmers, and the functioning core of IBM's 360 line of mainframe computers that provided single mainframe architecture for the entire set of computers and thereby a migration path for users, and IBM's long global dominance.[35]

The internet too was a Pentagon creation, the proudest success of Defense Advanced Research Projects Agency, DARPA. DARPA was created just after *Sputnik* to develop technology for the military. It was deliberately meant to be different— blue-sky, wild-eyed and wild, taking big risks, and thinking outside the box—and that's how it functioned, despite drawing fire for irrelevant wastefulness from Senator William

Proxmire, and others.[36] DARPA has been, arguably, America's most successful venture capitalist.

The internet's maiden name was the DARPANET. Behind the internet is the development, in the early 1960s of packet switching by Pentagon-funded researchers. Packet switching, now the dominant mode of communications routing, differs fundamentally from the traditional telephone circuit switching. Circuit switching provides a dedicated (temporary) circuit connection; packet switches break up a message into small "packets" that can be sent to a given destination any which way; they don't need a dedicated circuit. A communications network of packet switches, unlike one of circuit switches, needs no central control centers. But packet switching requires an extra layer. What a circuit-switched network does in hardware—that is, making the circuit—a packet-switched network must do in software. The circuit-creation software protocols that enable today's digital civilization are the twinned TCP/IP, developed not by some young venture-financed, garage-dwelling Silicon Valley engineer, but by Vinton Cerf, employed at DARPA, and Robert Kahn, who later headed DARPA.

DARPANET was turned into ARPANET—*defense* was dropped in preparation for its unveiling to the public—and grew to support orders-of-magnitude higher traffic when NSF funded the NSFNET—the high-volume "backbone" that enabled mass use. The creation of which it is indeed the case that then-Senator Al Gore importantly took the initiative.[37]

But a packet-switched network with a high-capacity backbone plus transmission-control and internetworking software that stay close to the bare metal and the bare sand are still of little use to anybody save computer scientists. What is needed are good, simple straightforward interfaces for both network users and resource creators. The hypertext markup language—HTML—provided both in one package. HTML was built at CERN, just on the Swiss side of the French border. CERN was anything but a free-market start-up, with dreams of profits and capital gains. CERN was and is a subatomic physics supercollider research laboratory run by a consortium of European governments. Like the other fundamental innovations, HTML was not written in Silicon Valley garages, but by another government bureaucrat: Timothy Berners-Lee. And the initial work on the first mass-market browser, then-called NCSA Mosaic, was carried out at another public-sector research laboratory, the National Center for Supercomputing Applications, by Marc Andreesen. The browser was then carried back, along with its creators, to Silicon Valley by entrepreneur Jim Clark, rewritten from scratch as a compatible clone, and then launched as the breakthrough IPO of the 1990s tech bubble: you know it as Netscape.

We have not cherry-picked in telling this story.

We could have spoken of how the mouse, icons, and point-and-click technology came out of PARC (Palo Alto Research Center—a research arm of the then–photocopying monopoly, Xerox). We could talk about how these were taken out the back door rather than the front door by the likes of Steve Jobs, who ran with them with great success. And we would note that later on Apple found it advisable to purchase from Xerox the intellectual property it had been deploying for decades.

We could have quoted Mariana Mazzucato on how the Apple iPhone consists overwhelmingly of government-created technologies that are artfully—with true genius—integrated, assembled, and displayed.[38] We could recount many other spin-off successes such as artificial intelligence, speech recognition, and satellite technology. We could speak of how pharmaceuticals too show their heavy dependency on government-financed R&D: Mazzucato cites studies showing that about 75 percent of new molecular entities—that is, actual new and not slight variants or "me too" drugs—came out of government-supported research.[39]

But the point is clear. It was the Pentagon, NASA, and other government agencies that did most of the work in creating and paying for the fundamental technologies of the digital age. And it was a host of entrepreneurs, founders of companies that are now rather large indeed, who took these inventions and platform technologies. They adapted them for multifarious, previously unimagined applications. And they thus redesigned the American economy.

The Long Age of Ike is a splendid example of America's recurrent history of government using whatever means it can muster that fit the situation—changing laws and regulations, extending the wherewithal—in cash, tax advantages, or risk-reducing insurance—to enable huge investments, providing protection against imports, supporting invention and technological development in many (and some very direct) ways, and combinations of all of these policies to open a new economic space. And when this new economic space has been created, opening it to a rush of entrepreneurial energy and innovations, which hugely expands its range and reshapes the economy.

But this long history of success of government's reshaping the economy by prodding, protecting, and enabling private enterprise to surge into new economic spaces, though perhaps no longer part of American memory and discourse, was not lost on the governments of other countries, who set about reshaping and developing their economies, and in the process, reshaped the American economy.

Chapter 4

The East Asian Model

It is not wrong to say that the East Asian development model was invented in the United States. Central to it is the concept of the *development state*, and, in the words of *Financial Times* columnist Martin Wolf: "It was America and Hamilton that invented that idea."[1] Pioneered by Hamilton, implemented in the late-nineteenth century by Bismarck's Germany, transplanted to East Asia by Japan, adopted by Korea, and then—with significant variations and at world-reshaping scale—by China, the East Asian development model has delivered unprecedentedly rapid growth and transformative development.[2]

It has also, as a byproduct, reshaped the American economy.

In the *developmental state*, government acts as far more than a mere referee, impartially enforcing the rules of competitive markets and accepting their outcomes, as in standard market theory and textbooks. Government is a player. Government actively organizes, enables, and directs industrial development. It is the partner of business, especially big or organized business. It doesn't necessarily own or run companies, though in some cases it does. It doesn't try to outlaw or supplant markets. It uses them.

Despite significant national differences, the goal was the same: not to invent the nation's future, but to catch up with it. The objective was to steer investment into industries that would pay off over the long run. It is not to direct resources into industries that earn the largest immediate profits for businesses at some set of current Smithian free-market prices. The object is to direct resources to industries that will pay off in terms of economic development. The idea is to use the market to provide businesses with incentives to skate to where the puck will be, not to where the puck is.

In more technical language, the object is to change over time the structure of the nation's comparative advantage, to go from being a producer of low-wage, low value-added, light manufacturing goods (cheap clothes, toys, and luggage)—or, worse yet, peasant agriculture—to a producer of the advanced goods that define an advanced nation: steel, ships, industrial machinery, autos, and electronics. It is to build communities of engineering and technological practice in which spillovers in knowledge—linkages horizontal, backward, and forward—will greatly amplify productivity.[3]

Can such policies go wrong? Yes. Can attempts to pursue such policies produce horrible economic disasters? In many cases they have. A catchphrase of development economist

Lant Pritchett is: "There are few things worse than state-led development carried out by an anti-developmental state."[4] It is a rare country that has not appealed to examples of successful developmental state-led economic growth to justify its own policies aimed at creating monopoly rents for the politically powerful.[5] Successful operation of the levers of economic policy in the interest of growth is relatively rare worldwide—but it is something that pre-1914 Germany had, that Japan and the rest of the East Asian Pacific Rim gained, and that China has acquired since 1980. It requires a government with a strong degree of insulation from and relative autonomy with respect to the desires of its countries' own plutocrats and organized corporatist interest groups to successfully design and execute such policies—but that is something that the United States, since Hamilton, has possessed.

Catching Up with the Future versus Inventing It

There is no reason to think that the economic organization that proved best at inventing an unknown industrial future is the one best suited to catching up with a known one.

The King of England did not call a meeting of barons, bishops, bankers, and a few mechanics and say: "Let's have an Industrial Revolution." Because the venture was genuinely new, the Smithian market was the right structure. It provided a try-and-see space with ample room for free play. Free markets thus succeeded not only at inventing wholly new technologies that became giant industries, but at inventing the very idea of industrial development.

But "call a meeting to say: 'let's have an Industrial Revolution'"—that is pretty much what Japan did.

Much of our economic thinking has been formed by the primal British case. Yet, for a significant portion of the world, it has not proven to be the best approach. Follower countries do not need to explore the economic space. They can see where they should go: they can see, in the economic structure of their richer neighbors, what manner of organization is adapted best to using new and advanced technologies. The economist who put it most pithily was Karl Marx: "The country that is more developed industrially only shows, to the less developed, the image of its own future."[6]

Follower countries' development strategies focus in a single-minded way on catching up with an economic future consisting of technologies, routines, products, and know-how invented and developed in other places at other times. They need to climb onto the very visible development trajectory that comes with those technologies' exercise and mastery that other, richer, countries have already achieved.

And who knows?—perhaps some variant of the East Asian state-led development model might prove to be very good indeed at innovation. Government, after all, played a leading role in driving invention and innovation in the United States during World War II and in the long postwar period. Problems of how to properly design economies to promote and manage economic growth are complex and knotty. But we do know almost surely, because the keys to economic growth in the last analysis are *ideas*, because *ideas* are both *non-rival* and *non-excludible*, and because all of economists' proofs of the optimality of the Smithian competitive market rely on the *rivalry* and *excludability* of commodities, that *laissez-faire* policies are not always the best approach.[7]

The jury is still out on East Asian innovation, but its verdict is clear on catch-up development: the East Asian development model works wondrously.

The East Asian model has nothing in common with the Stalinist model, where as a matter of ideology the economy was kept autarkic, walled off from international markets and world prices—indeed from prices altogether—and the state bureaucratically ran it as one giant conglomerate.

Like Hamiltonian America, and like Imperial Germany, East Asian governments have been pragmatic, providing very, very cheap capital to industries chosen as developmental and export performers; helping them get foreign technology, especially when the getting was not easy or the offer not altogether forthcoming; and providing protection against foreign competition. They don't typically own or directly manage firms—with the exception of China, where the beginning condition was total state ownership and where the growth, marketization, and partial privatization of state-owned firms has also been an important part of the process of transforming the Communist-Party *nomenklatura* of the civil service and its children into a market-economy *bourgeoisie* of bosses and entrepreneurs.[8]

The East Asian model doesn't do away with competition or international markets as an instrument to promote performance and innovation; it concentrates on its firms meeting the standards of competitive success in highly contested international markets, with a little help when needed. And they are anything but autarkic.

The East Asian development states have been enthusiastic—compulsive—trading nations, but not open, free-trade economies. Imports of product, investment, and corporate operations were carefully controlled, and not just by formal devices at the border such as tariffs, quotas, and licenses. Exchange rates were manipulated, and an undervalued exchange rate is a powerful positive lever of industrial development—as long as relatively low import shares keep the adverse terms-of-trade effects small as long as export-demand elasticities are favorable, and as long as the implicit protection against foreign competition thus produced is not allowed to keep alive firms so unproductive that they cannot export.

Nontariff barriers played critical roles: specific stories of protection, promotion, and organization in first one particular industry, then another strongly suggest that the bird's-eye view of key macro aggregates misses a huge part of the picture. Nor can this perspective address the very particular trade patterns of the East Asian states—strikingly different from those of the liberal economies of Europe and America—and their particular impacts on the rest of the world, especially the United States, long their target export market.

Tragedy and Comedy on the Economics Stage

Teaching tragedy—Sophocles, Euripides, and Shakespeare—even, alas Racine—is much easier and more common than teaching comedy—Aristophanes, Terence, and Sheridan. Why? Tragedy's few core truths apply in all circumstances, in all places, at all times: pride, greed, imbalances of passion and control. Tragedy can be set in Ancient Greece, Elizabethan England, or even modern Los Angeles. It can be staged in period costumes or even black T-shirts and blue jeans. The particularities don't much matter.

Comedy is all about context—circumstance, particularity, surprise, and inversion. The classics of comedy fall with a thud to our current crop of students, as they did to their parents and even grandparents.

The East Asian model has elements of both. There are, first, the few but powerful universals of tragedy and macroeconomics: high rates of savings and investment sustained of GDP (though, of course, their absolute levels can rise smartly). It also implies squeezing, or repressing returns to savers—a hidden tax—and shifting those returns to the industrial companies who access those savings. This means investment and exports drive growth. Year after year, investment grows faster than GDP and output faster than consumption. This means export surpluses, in part sustained by undervalued exchange rates—giving subsidies to foreigners who purchase the exports in the hope that human and organizational capital improvements via economies of scale and learning-by-doing will outweigh the cost of the implicit subsidies. And, indeed, as long as an under-valued exchange rate does not rob domestic businesses of their ability to obtain the first-world-produced capital goods and first-world-invented technology that they need, exchange rate undervaluation and manufacturing export orientation have since WWII led industrial development, increasing levels of sophistication in skills, in product and production, in logistics, and in marketing extending down the local supply and value chain.

Thus the East Asian fast development model is predicated on other nations—especially the United States—operating on a different, open economy model, absorbing those exports, running trade deficits, accepting the shrinking, and at times even the decimation, of major targeted industries. For one side, this means piling up large debts, conveniently in dollars that return one way or another into the American financial system. It means large financial flows, profitably intermediated to an important extent by America's financial firms. For the other side, it means accumulating ever-growing masses of dollars. It means accepting the high risk of their eventual depreciation against its own currency. It also means ever-bigger structural imbalances, between more and more debt-financed investment and lagging consumption. But, if it all works at the macroeco-nomic level, the structural imbalances are at an ever-higher level of productivity, sophistication, wealth, and income, and their resolution still leaves the economy way ahead.

These macroeconomic factors have powerful explanatory power.[9] But a good deal of what made the East Asian model, in its several national versions, so successful and so special in its impacts on the economies of its primary export markets is not encompassed in those few fundamental principles—high levels of savings at repressed interest rates; high investment; low consumption; repressed exchange rates and export surpluses. Nor do they shed any light on the unusual pattern of trade in the major export industries of the East Asian nations and the resultant difference in the impacts on their trading partners.

Here the comedy approach—call it micro, but perhaps *institutional* is a more accurate term—a focus on context, policy, and institutions comes into its own, and nowhere quite so clearly as Japan, the pioneer.

Japan

The first powerful success of the Asian development model, in many ways its modern invention, was Japan. During the thirty-five years beginning in 1955, when the Japanese economy was again as strong as it had been on December 7, 1941—aided by a boost from American procurement during the Korean War—and shortly after Germany and France had returned to prewar highs, growth for the next twenty years was the fastest the world had ever seen. Mind-boggling. From 1960 to 1973, the Japanese economy sustained a 10 percent per year average growth rate, quadrupling the economy in a short sprint and raising GDP per capita from 25 percent that of America to 57 percent. From 1973 to 1990—despite oil shocks, Reagan's 50 percent devaluation of the dollar against the yen, and American quotas on imports of Japanese automobiles (voluntary export restraints)—GDP grew at an average rate of 4.5 percent, doubling the economy and bringing Japanese per capita GDP up to 78 percent of America's.[10]

If you drop out differences in spending on prisons, defense, financial intermediation, the processing of medical insurance claims, and lawyers, the effective Japanese GDP per capita gets closer to the American. Of course, that in turn should be adjusted down for Japan's overstaffed and overpriced retail sector and the protections afforded to rice farmers, melon growers, and the like. International comparisons are difficult to make real.

Nevertheless, this was the highest sustained rate of growth of a big, real economy in the previous history of the world. A triumph. And Japan's success did not go unnoticed by its neighbors like Korea and Taiwan, who—unlike many Western economists—carefully studied what made it work and then set out, in true Japanese-style, to reverse engineer the miracle.

Japan, unlike Korea or China, did not enter its postwar high growth period as a preindustrial nation of dirt-poor, illiterate peasants. Japan had begun its government-guided industrialization in the nineteenth century in response to the arrival of America's Commodore Perry and his "black ships" (as the Japanese called them), with their big black cannons, intent on trading with, or exploiting, Japan. The political revolution of the Meiji restoration enabled Japan to respond to the menace of being colonized or subordinated; indeed, it was the only East Asian nation to escape that miserable fate (which it soon viciously imposed on other peoples). Japan set out to produce its own cannons and guns, to create "fukoku kyōhei": "a rich country and a strong army."[11] Its best and brightest were sent off to Europe and the United States to learn the new industrial skills, technologies, methods, and attitudes and to bring them back to Japan. By the end of 1941, it was clear that it had worked.

After World War II, there was a demolished industrial core to resurrect, not create. As the Cold War set in, and China fell to communism, the keystone of American policy in East Asia became Japan as a prosperous, democratic, and unsinkable ally, base, and example of how much better life could be outside the Iron Curtain. Japan's industrial policy regime was not questioned by America. At the beginning, in the 1950s and 1960s, it was painless for the unrivaled American economy. Even later, when Japanese exports started first to erode and then decimate the American industrial core, the US government continued to largely ignore moans and cries of "foul" from Pittsburgh, then Detroit, and then even Silicon Valley.

Why, one asks, did the United States not use the very considerable muscle it had at the time to open Japanese markets and protect its own? The pre–World War II American economy had been very good at protecting politically powerful domestic interests, after all.

Cold War strategic thinking was the major consideration.

In the troubled and troubling East Asia region, Japan had to be prosperous to be politically stable, and tightly tied to the United States. This attitude was bolstered by the more general American commitment to open trade left over from the Great Depression. The closing-off of world trade was seen as a major cause of the downturn, and was to be avoided. Moreover, free trade was good: we were the overwhelmingly dominant, the invincible economic as well as military and political superpower; open trade leads to prosperity and democracy; and free trade was good in itself. And, perhaps, from the viewpoint of Reagan and his successors, unionized and Democratic Rust-Belt manufacturing was not supposed to be among the high-value industries of America's future. Finance was. So when America finally pushed hard to open Japanese markets to American firms, it concentrated on finance.

The micro structures of Japan's high-growth economy involved at least four institutions:

- Protectionism not just at the dock but also through an intricate network of nontariff and social barriers

- The *keiretsu* system of interlocking corporate control and preferential industrial relationships

- A highly competent and politically insulated industrial policy bureaucracy

- Financial repression that kept rates of savings high, returns to savers low, and channeled very low-cost capital to targeted industries

Other factors can be added as well: education and skills; low crime rates; innovation in complex assembly; low military expenditures; a culture emphasizing meticulousness and collective obligation; a lawyer-free environment; and extreme social homogeneity. They all mattered. How much did each? If we knew that, we could teach comedy.

This institutional model was fit the high-growth period of 1955 to about 1990. Thereafter things changed. Japan had become a solidly rich nation. Japan had caught up with the most advanced economies. Japan had been forced to double the yen in exchange value. Asset values then crashed and stayed crashed; birth rates plummeted and stayed plummeted and the population started to age and shrink; the economy was opened up, dismantling many of those structural institutions; and rapid growth, or just about any nominal growth became dishearteningly elusive. Why? We do not claim to know.[12]

Economists oppose protectionism because it hurts consumers by increasing prices while benefitting producers who have done nothing productive to earn it. An industrial ecology of protectionism produces firms that are good at getting what they want out of government, but bad at running efficient current operations and improving technology. The rapid rise of Japanese consumption standards and the world-class performance in international markets of the major Japanese industrial firms, the beneficiaries of years of protection, provides evidence that this is not exactly how it worked in Japan.

Japan's protectionism did have elements of the classic story. For example, protecting rice-growing was seen as a necessary price that industrial development had to pay to buy off small farmers and the politicians who served them. Overall, on the evidence, Japanese protectionism was smart. At any particular moment, protectionism, along with financial repression, sacrifices the welfare of consumers to the benefit of producers. Yet over time, there were sufficient productivity gains to producers that even though at every moment consumer welfare was systematically unmaximized—sometimes gallingly so—it worked. Overpaying for most everything, they grew rich.

Economists don't like concrete cases—mere anecdotes, as they call them. They like data. But automobiles are not a mere anecdote when it comes to understanding the stellar performance of the Japanese economy. In 1960, Japanese-made automobiles were pathetically inferior to foreign brands such as Ford or Volkswagen. Yet there were essentially no imported automobiles in Japan. Ten years later, still zero. Ten years after that, still zero. For the forty postwar years, imports never captured more than 1 percent of the Japanese market.

Trade among the North Atlantic nations was significantly intrasectoral: nations that were major auto exporters were also significant auto importers; same for steel and machinery. For Germany, France, and the United States, most of the top ten exporting industries also ranked high among the top importing industries. There were some stark exceptions: military aircraft for the United States and wine and wheat for France.

Japan was different—very different. Japanese trade was not intrasectoral. In not one of its top ten export industries did Japan import in appreciable volumes.[13] Intrasectoral trade is different; it is far less disruptive. The difference changed the character of trade, making it into a game of wipeouts for its trading partners. As industries tend to cluster geographically, the result was the sudden creation of Rust Belt towns, first steel towns, then machinery towns, and then automobile cities.

Japan kept out not only foreign-made goods, but also foreign companies. Direct foreign investment was a key factor in damping the disruptions of international trade inside the North Atlantic.[14] The likes of Unilever, Procter & Gamble, Phillips, Ford, Fiat, Goodyear, Nestlé, and Gillette produced substantially in every advanced market—except Japan. As late as 1988 foreign companies produced about 1 percent of industrial output in Japan, while they produced close to 30 percent in France, 25 percent in Germany, and about 12 percent in the United States.[15] And those same Japanese firms—firms such as Toyota, Kawasaki, Komatsu, and Canon—that were protected against imports produced abroad and against foreign companies producing in Japan soon became world-class and world-conquering.

Behind most of the best firms was a *keiretsu*, an institutional form of industrial grouping and cross-holding that had no exact equivalent, or even rough approximation, in America or Europe. They were huge and omnipresent. The Mitsubishi *keiretsu*, for example, had major positions in banking, insurance, real estate, import-export houses (*shoga-shosha*), beer, electronics, oil, machinery, chemicals, pharmaceuticals, glass, plastics, department stores, paper, steel, shipping, automobiles, heavy industry, and many others. The group's sales equaled the GDP of a prosperous middle-sized country. The Sumitomo and Mitsui *keiretsu* were quite similar. In the mid-1980s, the top six *keiretsu* purchased three-fifths of all intermediate goods.[16] Aggressively funding and favoring "family" companies to develop their industrial capacity so that they could then "buy Japanese" provided a strong inner ring of protectionism.

Highly competent bureaucrats are needed to successfully run such an industrial policy, and Japan had them. Americans see government bureaucracy through the awful green wall paint, long lines, and dull, repetitive tasks. This image is an important part of how Americans have been taught to see the government. Bureaucracy looked different in Japan, not as the DMV or Post Office but as the levers of industrial policy: the elite ranks of the Japanese economics bureaucracy attracted the very top graduates of the top universities; bureaucrats were the best and the brightest; recruitment was honestly meritocratic; corruption was rare; salaries were in line.

And meritocratic selection was coupled with discretionary power. The ranking bureaucrats were very well informed about the industries they oversaw, and the vast range of assistance and controls at their disposal did not have to be applied, as a question of law, equally. But conflict with business was not the structuring principle. The cornerstone of industrial policy was the conviction that what was good for Mitsubishi or Sumitomo was good for Japan, and that the state was to guide, enable, and accelerate their development in its preferred directions. Formal specific laws, rules, and targets were kept to a bare and vague minimum. And like the French system, or the Pentagon system, ranking Japanese bureaucrats would retire to take very-well-paid positions in the companies they had overseen. The bureaucrat overseeing an industry would deal with his former boss who would soon again be critical to his next career move. That made conversation and cooperation all the easier.

By and large, politicians kept out of policy for the industrial core. They went elsewhere: the rent-seeking logic of politics governed agriculture, wholesale and retail trade, and construction. These were industries that did not have to face international competition, and they employed many more people than export-oriented manufacturing. In turn, the industrial policy technocrats stayed far away from those sectors, though they levied enormous costs on the Japanese economy. Small shops were protected. Costs to consumers were high. But so was employment, and neighborhoods retained their activity and intimacy—which was part of keeping Japan Japanese. There were no immigrants (and there still aren't). Protection raised Japanese prices for rice to about eight times world prices. The small rice farmers survived. They voted for costly protection so they could continue to make a (not very good) living via ten hours a day of stooping labor during planting season. But Japan was not and is not the only industrialized rich country with absurd levels of agricultural subsidy.

During the high-growth period, Japan maintained an extraordinarily high rate of savings, averaging above 30 percent of GDP, to match the very high rate of gross fixed investment.[17] Designated institutions, particularly the postal savings system, for a long time the world's biggest till, channeled capital to normal public works and rather a lot to politicians' infrastructural boondoggles as such specialized financial institutions do in many countries. Housing did not get the exceptional tax subsidies and other advantages that it received in the United

States. Indeed, the goal was to divert the flow of savings away from housing and toward industry. Repressed rates of return to savers did not discourage savings. You had to save for your old age. You had to save up a substantial down payment in order to buy a house. And there is little reason to assume that higher interest rates paid to savers induces higher rates of savings; the opposite often applies. The lower the return, the more you have to save for a targeted purpose. Seeking higher returns by placing savings abroad was successfully discouraged. Of course, no foreign-based financial institutions were permitted to operate in Japan until well after the high-growth period.

As Paul Krugman wrote back in 1987, "Ever since the development of the 'new trade theory' the case for free trade as the best policy has irretrievably lost its innocence. Its status has shifted from optimum to reasonable rule of thumb. There is still a case for free trade as a good policy, and as a useful target in the practical world of politics, but it can never again be asserted as the policy that economic theory tells us is always right . . . "[18]

In Krugman's view, there are four reasons why free trade remains good policy and a useful target in the practical world of politics. They are:

- Attempts to craft successful internationally-oriented industrial policies—those that grab a larger share of increasing-return sector-specific rents or a larger share of learning-by-doing and other spillovers—are highly likely to call forth retaliation and trade war, and end in a truly bad equilibrium of limited, administered trade.

- To figure out what really are the industries of the future—what industries do promise large rents and high spillovers in the future—is, for standard Hayekian information reasons, beyond the competence of bureaucrats to calculate.

- Rent-seeking interests can easily deploy the rhetoric of industrial policy to convince governments to adopt not positive-sum but negative-sum interventions. Ideal technocratic guardians in Plato's Republic could conduct developmental industrial policies successfully; our rulers and bureaucrats cannot. As Cicero complained to his best friend back in the first century BC, we find ourselves living "not in the Plato's Republic but in Romulus's sewer."[19]

- Even successful industrial policies build economically powerful and politically canny interests that then keep the policies subsidizing them going long-past the sell-by date: better not to get into the business in the first place.[20]

But what if your transoceanic trading partner—for Cold War strategic reasons and as part of taking steps toward building a climate of freer trade worldwide—does not wish to retaliate and so risk destructive trade war? And what if you are not trying to invent the future but merely to catch up to your future—which is already the present of the superpower across the great ocean to your east? And what if your bureaucrats are actually more akin to the guardians of Plato's Republic than to the corrupt rent-seekers of Romulus's sewer—at least until Japan had caught up with the world economic leaders, and the system began to change out from under them?

These are powerful concerns. Growth has stilled in Japan. Economic historians will explain why and economic pundits will trumpet cautionary warnings. But nothing will erase the fact that if your overriding national objective as of 1950 was the most rapid convergence to as close as possible to North Atlantic living standards and productivity levels, Japan designed its economy via its post–World War II industrial policy to do that job, and do it very well.

If this chapter of the book had not already grown beyond its proper size given our overall architecture, we would now turn to discussions of astonishing growth in South Korea, of the success of the Guomindang at creating a developmental state in Taiwan, of the marvelous two city-states of Hong Kong and Singapore, and of Malaysia, Indonesia, and Thailand, where growth has been impressive relative to much of the rest of the developing world but disappointing compared to the East Asian Pacific Rim proper. But we must take all that as read, and turn to China.

China

China, with its system-bursting scale, has pushed the model to its limits and perhaps beyond. A first limit to the developmental-state model is external: the capacity and willingness of other countries to absorb its exports, to pile up debt, and to tolerate the shrinking of manufacturing out of not just the low-value-added industries of their industrial past (most everything at Walmart or Target) and the present (steel, ships, cranes, pumps, compressors, small appliances, bigger appliances), but what had been thought to be the cutting-edge manufacturing industries of their future (solar panels, LEDs, networking equipment, supertrains). A second limit is domestic: the high-wire act of shifting the drivers of growth from investment and exports financed by cheap debt to domestic consumption, especially services. China's new top leadership has publicly stated that it understands how China is rubbing against the limits, and that it will act to restructure. But saying is not acting. And acting is not doing.

China disciplined itself to the macro levers of the basic East Asian model: high rates of savings, repressed rates of returns to savers, high rates of investment, low rates of consumption, export surpluses. And its sustained performance in each of these macro drivers has been more than extraordinary. Investment in China has climbed to 50 percent of GDP.[21] This level is off the curve—two-thirds again higher than Japan in its high-growth period. Savings have kept pace. Exports have climbed to 30 percent of GDP. Consumption has been repressed to only 34 percent of GDP, also off the curve, this time at the bottom.

The "comedy," or institutional and sector-specific policy components of the growth model, have been different for China and Japan. China started on its trajectory of economic reform and rapid development as a miserably poor peasant economy. It had just seen the ebbing of another wave of economic and social destruction, wrought by a ruthless and apparently mad totalitarian Great Leader: Great Leaps Forward, Great Sparrow Campaigns, Great Locust Plagues, Great Famines, and Great Proletarian Cultural Revolutions. It was Deng Xiaoping—finally, pragmatically, sensibly stating that what one cared about in a cat was not whether it was revolutionarily red or reactionarily white, but whether it caught mice—who set China on what has proven to be an unimaginably successful trajectory of structural economic reform.

And since his adventure in reform began in the late 1970s the Chinese economy's growth has astonished the world.

At the beginning, reforms were tentative: controllable experiments in bounded areas that could be shut down swiftly without having contaminated the vast red rest of China. There was no shared consensus on just how far-reaching reform would be or where it would lead. There was a mere choice of direction: *not* the Soviet Union, *not* the cult of personality, and somehow *toward* the successes of the fast-growth Asian Pacific Rim economies, all to be called "Socialism with Chinese characteristics."

Reform began with agriculture, which directly employed about three-quarters of the Chinese workforce in 1978. Communes were dismantled. Peasants got their farms back with enough security of tenure to encourage investment in irrigation, drainage, breeding stock, and equipment. Peasants were told that they had to continue to sell to the state the same quantities as they sold to the state the previous year at the same state set price, but they could sell anything beyond that at market prices. Few economists would have counseled such a dual-price structure with its built-in promise of black market corruption. But rising output quickly trivialized the assigned quotas and the corrupting force of the dual-track pricing system.

Agricultural output grew smartly, compounding at about 5 percent per year, and so more than doubled by 1995 while the agricultural workforce fell by a quarter, down to 53 percent.[22] Peasants saw that they were living three times as well as they had in the bad old days of Mao Zedong. That gave the regime of Deng Xiaoping and his successors enormous street credibility.

Stalin's greatest and most murderous failure was his brutally forced collectivization of agriculture. It was intended to enable the state to control agricultural output (and the peasants) and take it (and the peasants' sons) off the farm to build the dams, roads, electrification, and factories of the Five-Year Plans. It kept Soviet agriculture a lagging sector for generations, employing vastly more than its normal share of the labor force at productivity incredibly low even by Soviet standards. It turned the Ukraine from a grain-exporting region rivaling the US Midwest into an economic drain.

Similarly, forced collectivization under Mao had failed to generate increases in agricultural output and productivity to support industrialization. Deng and his reformers inverted the model and succeeded: shifting peasants out of low-, often zero-productivity work in agriculture and into factories—manufacturing goods with machines.

But who in China could buy the output of these factories? The peasants had no money. Effective domestic demand could increase only slowly, too slowly for rapid industrial growth. Only exports could absorb the output and grow its volume vertiginously, yield rich gains of learning-by-doing—the very essence of real development—promote improvement in its quality and sophistication, and provide the foreign exchange to purchase the machines needed for sustaining that expansion and upgrading. That, after all, is the obvious lesson China could read from the high-growth economies of East Asia: Japan and Korea, Singapore and, yes, Taiwan.

But who would teach the Chinese how to produce, as well as provide the know-how, technology, and access to foreign markets? A bold and rather fundamental reform addressed this question. It came as a near-universal surprise: Communist China opened its economy to foreign companies—indeed, eagerly courted them. Foreign companies would bring technology, know-how, access to export markets, and even capital. Of course, they had to be kept on a tight chain, carefully supervised, and made to contribute what they had to the Chinese economy.

This bold departure was begun cautiously, experimentally. Delimited geographic areas were made into special economic zones, opened to controlled foreign investment. The first was just across from Hong Kong. The next, across from Taiwan. Then one up further north near to Japan. Again, if things threatened to get out of hand, the zones could be quickly closed. China had very bitter memories indeed of foreign enclaves.

At the beginning, there was no way indigenous Chinese firms would know what kind of garments or toys to make for the outside world; nor would they know how to make them efficiently and to world standards; nor could they, by themselves, market and sell them. The Hong Kong people brought those things to the party, and it was very valuable. Hong Kong apparel, shoe, toy, and garment companies led the way, setting up sewing and light-assembly factories. China supplied very cheap labor and the guarantee of labor discipline. The native fluency in Cantonese of the "foreigners," their Han faces, their family ties, and the obvious fact that Hong Kong was not in itself a potentially threatening ex-colonial power should not disguise the enormous importance of China opening itself.

The US-China Trade Balance

The lopsided US-China trade balance is a politically charged topic in the United States, where politicians and journalists demand substantial revisions of the RMB-dollar exchange rate held artificially low by China. The year 2011 saw $129 billion of US exports to China and $411 billion of US imports from China—a net $282 billion deficit, at that far below its mid-2000s peak. In the depressed US economy of 2011, balanced trade with China would have been worth three million more jobs in the United States.

But conventional accounting applied to binational trade is marvelously misleading. The United States is China's biggest national export market; minuscule Hong Kong is second. More important, everything that goes out of China to the United States counts as a Chinese export, though its Chinese value added has just climbed up to perhaps half the total.[23] The analysis of the iPhone is the most famous example, with only $6.54 Chinese value added to an iPhone priced at $169.41 at the factory door, then selling for $599 when sold in the Apple store to the combination of the customer and AT&T.[24] China has been working steadily and successfully to increase the Chinese value added of its exports.

United States exports to China also change dramatically when seen in value-added terms. The quintessential US export—a Boeing 777 jet—has a foreign value added of about one-third, with Japan the major production "partner." The older Boeing 727 had foreign value-added of about 2 percent; the US too has been working steadily at changing the domestic value added of its exports.[25]

The OECD and the WTO are attempting to do the heavy lifting to track international trade by value added.[26] In their preliminary accounting, only about half of conventionally counted Chinese and American bilateral exports consist of Chinese and American value added, which implies a $141 billion bilateral deficit in value added instead of the $282 billion deficit in conventionally counted trade flows. Perhaps too neatly halved, but still substantial, economically as well as politically.

"Predatory" Investment

Technology transfer was central to China's plans for foreign firms, and it still is. Over half and possibly as much as two-thirds of Chinese exports during the past decade came from what the Chinese call *foreign-invested* companies.[27] And a very, very considerable part of Chinese firms' climb up the ladder of industrial sophistication came, one way or another, from foreign firms. Witness the latest, and to date grandest, examples: high-speed trains, solar panels, and networking equipment. Japan based its own rapid growth on a successful determination to keep foreign companies out. China invited them in, more and more openly and cordially, and used them to its own purpose ever more effectively. China turned out not to need foreign capital for very long; its own savings rate could finance things. What it needed, more and more, was foreign technology and know-how. All companies coming in to produce or sell, or both, were until quite recently required to have Chinese companies as partners. The Chinese partner would provide such valuable things as official permissions and permits and the connections necessary to access the Chinese market, bank financing, or just about anything else. But the partner was also there to make sure that technology and know-how that came into the joint venture quickly poured into Chinese hands.

Technology transfer moved up the ladder of sophistication very quickly, more quickly than outsiders could have imagined. The high-speed train built by Siemens to run the ludicrously short distance from the Shanghai airport into town was of course a demonstration product; behind it was the promise of a major piece for Siemens of what would be the world's biggest high-speed rail program. But inviting in the major high-speed train producers was the way for China to get the technology into Chinese hands, which it succeeded in doing with breathtaking speed—it is now the world's largest

producer (and buyer) of them.[28] Is there any company operating in China with an interesting technology that believes
it is not having its technology "homaged"—imitated, stolen?
The American Francis Cabot Lowell went to England to
frantically sketch the workings of British textile machinery.
When he returned to the United States, he brought along
British engineers such as John Moody who got equity kick-
ers in the new enterprises for turning the drawings into the
machines they remembered using. Pre-1789 *ancien régime*
France too was not above purloining important technology, in
this case the secrets of making fine Chinese porcelain, which
was smuggled out by French missionaries. It has been always
thus.[29]

At about 50 percent of GDP, China's investment spending has
reached a proportion that no other country has ever sustained or
even attained. Local governments play a big role in generating
and directing investment. Chinese local governments are not
like local governments (or even state governments) in the United
States or Europe. Of course, they provide basic services: roads,
water and sewers, transportation, police and fire, schools, and
the like. But Chinese local and provincial governments also play
a major role in promoting and steering industrial investment
and production. They are big—perhaps the biggest—players in
economic development, not just infrastructure and urban services, and their efforts are most poorly coordinated.

To promote growth and employment, they back or arrange
bank financing. When the loans can't be repaid, or repaid conveniently (in terms of sales and employment), they can, with
the help of the local government, be rolled over. They can even

be rolled over so generously that new borrowing covers current interest payments. Investment can be made to be close to costless. Local government can make land available to selected developers and companies on extremely favorable terms by seizing land at the ever-advancing urban edge at extremely unfavorable, below-market-value prices; that spread between seizure price and productive value is both a significant source of government financing and a way to enrich selected developers and companies—and officials and their families. Chinese officials seem to wind up with much richer families than their American or European counterparts. And growth keeps the mechanism going.

Local governments demand performance in return: growing sales and employment. There are a great many powerful local governments in China, and they compete with one another to foster growth. Their top officials also compete: they are promoted according to formal and informal performance metrics, high on the list of which are economic and employment growth.

Overinvestment can seem a distant threat when urban development has to accommodate well over ten million new urbanites a year and GDP grows at 10 percent per year. Consider the following, from an article that one imagines got a nod from the government:

> Since 2003 Beijing has issued at least three policy circulars ordering the aluminum industry to correct its overcapacity problem, caused by local governments' pursuit of their own interests. Ten years on the situation has not

improved and is expected to worsen for at least a few
more years . . . [30]

That is, ten years of splendid and successful resistance by
local governments to central government efforts to close down
the least efficient and most polluting smelters. But they use
large quantities of local coal, and China, the world's largest
coal miner, employs almost six million coal miners, as compared with the United States, the second-biggest coal miner,
which employs only eighty thousand. So the smelters stay. As
the Chinese proverb has it, "The mountains are very high, and
the Emperor is very far away." As Chinese capacity expanded
to 50 percent of world aluminum production capacity, triggering price collapses, foreign producers responded by crying foul
but also by shuttering capacity.

Container ships are massive pieces of capital that demand
little labor to operate. The new ones, the biggest yet, can carry
as many as eighteen thousand 20-foot containers. In the 1990s,
a giant carried five thousand. Ships ordered before the 2008
crash are now being delivered, and the industry is suffering
from overcapacity. And yet in the teeth of this global overcapacity, China Shipping Container Lines ordered five new
behemoths. The shipping line is not a big employer, but the
shipyards are. And financing didn't seem to be a problem.
Someone else who faces real capital costs will have to adjust.[31]

Solar panels are a poster-boy industry of the future, as Barack
Obama, Angela Merkel, and Silicon Valley venture capitalists
told us. World production of solar panels rose by 50 percent in
the five years beginning in 2004. Chinese production rose 400

percent. Well over 90 percent of that production was exported. Chinese output then rose by 1000 percent, between 2008 and 2012, mostly for export—so that the price of solar cells and modules plummeted by 75 percent.[32] The Chinese had more than 65 percent of the world market, putting American and European producers out of business. American producers filed their complaint with the US International Trade Commission, which duly imposed countervailing duties of 2.4–4.7 percent to offset subsidies, which was subsequently increased. Two days later, the European Union announced that it was opening an inquiry, but European producers of autos and luxury goods plus, of course, Airbus—all heavily dependent on the China market—pressured the EU to avoid antagonizing the Chinese government on trade matters. The EU dropped its case.

Something quite similar surrounded EU investigations of communications equipment, which meant Huawei and ZTE. At the insistence of the German government, the EU dropped its case.[33] Producing photovoltaic cells and modules or LED lighting is not a labor-intensive process; it is technology- and capital-intensive; that is China's job. Installing them on roofs is technology-light, capital-light, but labor-intensive—and fully safe from foreign competition; that is the job of America.

The Limits of the Model: Imbalances

Has China arrived at the limit of its growth model, as Japan did over twenty gray years ago? Many think it has.

Many macroeconomists see flashing cautionary indicators—some see time bombs—in the increasingly skewed proportions of GDP: consumption radically too low; investment too high, financed far too cheaply. The result is an accumulation of white elephants, unproductive investments, overcapacity, papered-over dud loans, and exports that can no longer grow at previous rates. Even the new top leadership has repeatedly called China's growth path "imbalanced and unsustainable."[34]

China responded to the world economic crisis and its hit on Chinese exports (the trade surplus had fallen by one-third between 2008 and 2009, over $100 billion) with an enormous 2008 stimulus, about $700 billion, 13 percent of GDP, mostly to finance investment. That pulled Chinese GDP growth up and away from the rest of the sagging world to 10.4 percent in 2010 and 9.3 in 2011. Total internal debt increased from about 150 percent of GDP in 2008, to about 250 percent by the end of 2014.

This debt level is still lower than that of the United States or Japan: even ever-frugal Germany's is about 200 percent. And it is not financed by foreign borrowings. Still, debt cannot grow at such a rate for very long, even in dollar-stuffed China. And rapid growth in overall debt, especially when accompanied by financial innovation—and China's financial sector has recently become quite innovative—is usually a dead-certain sign of even faster growth in imprudent lending and bad debt. There are schadenfreude-filled analogies to the miserable denouement of other high-leverage investment booms: Japan in the 1990s, the United States in 1929 and again in 2008, Spain in 2008.

What is needed is articulated, at the abstract level, by armies of analysts and commentators: rein in excess credit growth, cut the crony- and politically influenced loose lending, increase consumption, extend the social safety net, rid the Party and the system of corruption, and, especially, move decisively toward "more market and less state." Surprisingly to some, this is also the new mantra of China's top leadership. All in all, it is very concrete: more services, more safety net, less pollution, less heavy industry, and slower construction and infrastructure build-out. Quite understandable, quite concrete.

At the end of 2013, the leaders meeting at Party plenum—the very top leaders—set out these very goals in a bold and far-reaching reform agenda. There is every reason to take it seriously. It is a major political thrust. That, however, does not mean that China will succeed in implementing these major reforms at scale and in time.

One advantage China has, compared with most other nations facing troubling macro imbalances and a developing debt crisis, is that the powerful leadership is fully aware of the problems and of the likely consequences—the second- and even third-order effects of clever and bold first-order actions.

Where politics has convinced itself that it is hugely dependent on rapid growth, and where growth is hugely dependent on even faster growth in investment, and where rocketing investment has been fueled by more and more dicey debt, abruptly turning down the credit spigot risks triggering a balance sheet crash—a cure worse than the disease.

Liberalization of capital markets is the most powerful, but also the most risky of measures; it is often wildly headstrong.

In country after country, when the sluice gates were opened to capital flows, destabilizing excesses have been a more common experience than welcome increases in the efficiency of capital utilization. Still, Chinese capital markets are being permitted ever-greater liberty, scope, and influence. A fall off the high-growth trajectory triggered by a sudden drop in investment would be very destabilizing, and destabilization—economic destabilization, social destabilization and political destabilization—is the most important second-order consequence on the leadership's list.

Furthermore, all systems generate their share of wasteful investment, especially in boom times, and it has been super-boom time in China for thirty years. Traditional Chinese medicine is more likely than radical surgery.

A low-hanging fruit is reform of the *hukou* household registration system. It would affect 140 million migrant workers currently living in cities but excluded from social protections and services and working longer hours for lower wages because they lack residency permits. That would be a giant step toward a more just and equal society, and would also provide a big boost in rebalancing toward consumption as well as a likely reduction in the overheated savings rate. But it entails a huge jump in wage costs. Urban China is no longer cheap-labor China: wages have risen ten times faster than Mexican wages, and there has been a 50 percent plus appreciation of the RMB against the Mexican peso. China's wages are now higher than Mexico's.[35] What would a big wage jump do to Chinese export competitiveness? Should workforce formalization be combined with, say, exchange rate or capital market liberalization, multiplying the impact and the risk and setting everything spinning?

Regularization also implies a major change in local government financing. Currently, local governments pay the lion's share of social services—health and education—and they derive about 40 percent of their revenues from land transactions from the ever-overheated boom in real estate. Second-order considerations temper zeal as they cloud the laserlike clarity of the simple but powerful macro prescriptions. Laser focus is to be better trusted in cosmetology than in political economics. "Prudence" will be the guiding principle and "gradually" is its first derivative.

The problem is not, of course, disagreement from an opposition party, but rather resistance from entrenched interests within the Party and the business-based interests that the investment-led boom has created. Chinese income distribution is badly skewed toward the very top. The top 1 percent of households have one-third of the nation's wealth while the bottom third has about 1 percent.[36] And it is not very easy to disentangle Party officials, government officials, and business leaders. China is a society blessed by strong family ties, and the families of ranking officials have become very rich indeed. Recent revelations of the spectacular wealth of the very top leaders' families indicate the pervasive reach of corruption. China has created powerful, entrenched interests that stand in the way of the proposed reforms.

The new top leadership seems to be trying to seize control at the center. Economic liberalization may well imply political illiberalism. A move to more market and less state may well mean a more powerful and centralized state—at least for the short run. But a more centralized state may well try to stay that way.

Markets will take a more dominant role in the economy. Generalized overcapacity will be cut back, as will leverage. More Chinese will be integrated into formal employment, social protection and public schooling. But when, how, and how much are open questions as is the question of whether the landing will be only a bit bumpy or a crash, or something bigger and unknowable: after a generation at close to 10 percent GDP growth, a cruising speed of 7 percent, as the government indicates? More likely lower, say 6 percent? Even 5 percent? Significantly lower rates? Perhaps 4 percent a year. But as Ricardo Hausmann puts it, "the path from 8 percent growth to 4 percent growth often goes through negative 2 percent."[37]

———————

Whatever the macro adjustments, and they are likely to be major and unsettling, one thing is sure. The efforts of the state—at its various levels—to promote Chinese success in the industries of the future will not go away. China will not transform itself into an undirected free-market carnival. The government will continue its strategic efforts to upgrade and reshape the economy and that implies reshaping the American economy. How has America responded to these efforts by East Asian governments?

Chapter 5

The Hypertrophy of Finance

Now don't get us wrong. Finance is good. Finance is necessary.

We like low finance. It has obvious efficiencies. We like the ability to use banknotes, checks, credit cards, and electronic money rather than having to cart around chests of silver, scales to weigh metal, and reagents to assay the purity of what is offered, not to mention the armed guards needed to protect the silver (and more guards to watch the first set of guards). We like the ability of households to borrow and lend, so they are not forced to match income and expenditure every day, week, month, or year. We like the ability of businesses to finance receivables.

And we like high finance—but in its proper place.

We like the ability of entrepreneurs to raise capital to grow their businesses. We like the ability high finance gives them to share the immense risks of entrepreneurship

and enterprise. We like the potential for activist investors to curb the worst abuses of entrenched management,
through threatening or proceeding with takeovers to throw
the bums out. We like the ability of individual investors
to diversify their portfolios—and thus sleep easy because
they are insured, via diversification, against the risk that
something will go wrong with a company in which they
invested. We like the basic function of pooling individual
savings and allocating them, carefully, to companies seeking to invest and to homebuyers. All of these things, and
many more, are very good.

But all that could be done with a much smaller financial
sector than America now has. Indeed, it *was* done with a
much smaller financial sector than America now has. It was
not some wild-eyed Occupy drummer but rather former Fed
Chair Ben Bernanke who told *Financial Times* columnist
Martin Wolf that he couldn't disagree that the "more repressed
financial system" of the 1950s and 1960s—in addition to being
much, much cheaper for an economy to pay for—provided
significantly more safety without significantly hobbling real
economic growth.[1]

All that could be done and was done with the 3.7 percent of
the economy in the finance sector that, according to Thomas
Philippon, we had in the 1950s.[2] Today, the finance sector
accounts for more than 8.5 percent of the economy—and that
share is growing. What have we gotten from this that is worth
anything to the rest of us?

It is not some hippie but, instead, former Federal Reserve
chair Paul Volcker whose assessment is that the only

worthwhile innovation in finance in the past thirty years is the ATM.[3] And it was not some unsophisticated leftie, but Jack Bogle, the founder of Vanguard, the largest manager of index stock funds and now ETFs, who said:

> The job of finance is to provide capital to companies. We do it to the tune of $250 billion a year in IPOs and secondary offerings. What else do we do? We encourage investors to trade about $32 trillion a year. So the way I calculate it, 99 percent of what we do in this industry is people trading with one another, with a gain only to the middleman. It's a waste of resources.[4]

In the post–World War II years—the late 1940s into the 1970s—America had a system of finance that violated the strictures of free markets—that what was not regulated, or only lightly regulated, was best. It was byzantine and convoluted. It had all sorts of restrictions on who could own what. It had all sorts of restrictions on who could do what.

It seemed to have only one virtue: it worked. It successfully provided access to liquidity and savings vehicles for households and firms; allowed households to borrow long-term to purchase houses and so acquire skin in the game of maintaining these residences; had insurance arms that helped Americans sleep easy; enabled entrepreneurs to raise capital and to share the risks of enterprise; and made it straightforward for individual investors to diversify their portfolios. It did this at a not unreasonable cost and without destabilizing (or worse) financial crises.

But it involved an extraordinary degree of regulation of the market. Because of an appropriate fear that they would run outsized risks with government-insured money, commercial banks were forbidden from competing with an investment banking oligarchy that collected clearly outsized profits from what seemed a straightforward transaction business of securities issues and mergers. Portfolio managers found that if they sought a prudent-manager safe harbor in order to avoid potential legal trouble, they were restricted in the classes of assets they could invest in.[5] Banks and savings and loans were forbidden to offer interest on checking accounts—thus forcing them to compete on service and promotional toaster giveaways rather than cash value to depositors. Plus, there were ceilings on savings account interest rates. Leverage was restricted. And Delaware had bid for the legal business of corporations by offering managers a legal structure that made them all but invincible if they sought to hold on to their power and their soft compensation, no matter how poor their performance. Wherever any economist or free marketeer looked, the American financial system was riddled with government overregulation and interference.

Yet in spite of all this, the American economy grew faster and more smoothly than in the present era, with a higher ratio of real value to transaction intermediation and zero-sum claims processing. And the capital flowed.

Since then, American finance has been transformed.

Why and how has this happened? What has it meant for our economy?

The Growth of American Finance

Back in the old days, in the 1950s and 1960s and indeed in the Gilded Age in the last quarter of the nineteenth century, the cost of America's financial system—the fortunes of the plutocrats at the top plus the salaries of the paper-pushers who actually kept track of who owned what and tried to figure out what it was worth—amounted to perhaps 1.2 percent of total financial assets per year.[6] Today the cost of finance is much closer to 3 percent of total financial assets per year. And it is not at all clear that that cost is not still rising.

With the increase in the financialization of the economy, total financial assets are a larger multiple of GDP today than they were in the past. In the 1950s, total financial assets were on the order of two and a half years' worth of GDP. Today they are more than three years' worth. From the 1940s through the early 1980s, compensation in finance was pretty much the same as in other sectors. By 2007 it was four times as high.[7] (And the legions of tellers and clerks, whose ranks were reduced by Paul Volcker's uniquely favorite innovation in finance—the ATM—did not see their wages rise much. It all went up to the top.)

The rise in the scope of finance as measured by assets relative to the real economy and this rise in the cost of financial intermediation per dollar of assets are the two factors that have pushed our financial sector from somewhat under 4% to more than 8 percent of total income. This is a sectoral resource and income shift of nearly a full Pentagon.

For the first forty postwar years, profits to financial firms moved in a range of between 10 and 15 percent of total profits of publicly held corporations. By 1986, they hit 16 percent. And as financialization has spread and intensified, they have kept rising. They varied between 20 percent and 30 percent in the 1990s. By 2002, they passed 40 percent.[8] In 2007, at their peak they hit almost half. Since then they have retreated—but not even down to their 2002 level.

That staggering figure—almost half of total corporate profits for financial intermediation—significantly under-counts the reality of just how big a hunk of everything finance has taken. It doesn't include many financial firms that were not publicly held corporations—consider venture partnerships and private equity operations. It doesn't include the many wholly owned financing subsidiaries of industrial firms. Consider Jack Welch's GE, or Ford (the finance division of Ford was responsible for all the company's profits in 2002 and 2003). And it does not include the many financial companies that operate out of New York and Connecticut but are domiciled in tax havens like the Cayman Islands, so that their company earnings do not enter this accounting. Nor does it include big law and accounting firms that are an integral part of finance but are counted as professional services.

Aside from this finance-led massive redistribution of income to the very top, have the rest of us gotten anything out of this hypertrophy of finance?

Certainly we have not gotten faster commercial and indus-trial economic growth than in the 1950s and 1960s. Nor have we gotten more rapid structural economic transformation than in the 1880s or the 1960s. If the growth of finance has produced a better allocation of capital across industries and firms, it is not obvious how or where. If the growth of finance has produced managers who were better at keeping their eyes on the ball or a system that chooses better managers for large corporations, it is not obvious. As Thomas Philippon writes:

> Despite its fast computers and credit derivatives, the current financial system does not seem better at transferring funds from savers to borrowers than the financial system of 1910 . . . The finance industry of 1900 was just as able as the finance industry of 2010 to produce loans, bonds and stocks, and it was certainly doing it more cheaply. This is counter-intuitive, to say the least. How is it possible for today's finance industry not to be significantly more efficient than the finance industry of John Pierpont Morgan?[9]

The thumbnail answer is that there are now seven ways to make money in finance:

1. Find some operating-company potential venture that is still on the table and that has an attractive risk-return profile, and finance it.

2. Find some set of potential investors who would benefit in a risk-return sense for taking on the financing of operating-company ventures of which they are unaware, and make them aware.

3. Convince some set of investors that they should bear risks that they really ought not to bear, and so persuade them to take these risks off your hands.

4. Convince some set of investors that they should not bear risks that they currently are and should be bearing, and so persuade them to allow you to take these risks off their hands.

5. Buy fabulously fast computers and fiber optical connections, locate next to the exchange's computers and front run incoming orders; garner a tiny bit on each turn and do it again and again and again at breathtaking speed.

6. Manage an account actively with an eye to generating fees: fees for management; fees for buying and selling (and do lots of that); fees for managing the funds in which you place the assets; fees from investment funds in which you place your clients' funds.

7. Know something others don't or simply be lucky.

Some economists will tell you that there are societal benefits to engaging in (3), (4), and even (5). A financial market in which many participants do not understand the risks they are or should be bearing is one in which prices are pushed away from fundamental values. Relieving those "noise traders" of their money so that investments are made by those who do understand risk and return would produce a configuration of asset prices that would provide better signals to operating companies and better match private profit to societal well-being.

But that argument does not apply to the extent that financiers are spending time, energy, and other resources to take advantage of—indeed, often to create—the misperceptions of others. They are, as Nobel Prize–winning economists George Akerlof and Robert Shiller have written in their book of the same name, really in a business best described as *phishing for phools.*[10]

As Philippon has written:

> Technological improvements in finance have mostly been used to increase secondary market activities, i.e., trading. Trading activities are many times larger than at any time in previous history. Trading costs have decreased, but I find no evidence that increased liquidity has led to better (i.e., more informative) prices or to more insurance . . .[11]

The Impulse to Expand High Finance

The extraordinary rise in trading and other dissipative activities was a byproduct of incentives, information asymmetries, and human psychology set free to interact in new ways by the removal of financial regulations. It was not in and of itself an intended aim of government policy. It did, however, become the policy of the government to dismantle the long-serving regulatory framework that inhibited trading activity and to let the market govern. This was the result of a shift in national mood away from broad political support for tightly regulated—and relatively boring, if respectably remunerative—finance to one of deregulation and experimentation. This shift had a number of causes.

One was the simple ebbing of the memory of the financial crises of the pre-SEC era and the bank failures of the Great Depression. As Hyman Minsky famously wrote, a financial system that is successfully regulated in the interests of system stability generates enormous pressures to dismantle that regulation and allow gunslinger finance, for those who pressed the limit on taking risks—as long as the system remained stable—are seen to have profited immensely.[12] And so, come the 1970s, we here in America decided that we needed to redesign and "marketize" finance.

This was not purely a Right Wing or a Republican initiative. It was, in many of its pieces, a good-government initiative. Policymakers of both parties were enthusiastic about experimentation with new types of securities and new modes of financial business. For a century, after all, those who had been able to invest in the stock market or in real estate for the long term in America had by and large done very well, but not particularly well—nor particularly badly—during the 1960s, when the economy was robust, nor in the 1970s, when it wasn't. And policies that put barriers in the way of not-so-rich or not-so-sophisticated potential investors, whether those barriers were procedural or administrative on the one hand or psychological by scaring people with warnings of financial risks, seemed ripe for elimination. As time went on and imports ate away at manufacturing, America began to look at finance as a new growth sector and even a new export sector.

It began to focus trade negotiations on opening markets to its financial firms in exchange for easing the way for imports of foreign manufactured goods.

The Clinton Treasury (and one of us who worked in the Clinton Treasury) was relatively enthusiastic about the repeal of Glass-Steagall and the opening up of investment banking to competition from deep-pocketed commercial banks and insurers. This move was supposed to break the market power that old-line investment banks like Morgan Stanley had wielded to produce such outsized profits. If it in the process produced gigantic megabanks, the Federal Reserve had ample tools to make sure that economy-wide spending stayed stable, so that too-big-to-fail banks did not fail.

But it was not just the ebbing of the memory of the Great Depression that caused the shift. There was also a powerful ideological surge: the growing belief that, as Ronald Reagan put it, the "scariest words" you could hear were: "'I'm from the government, and I'm here to help you.'"[13]

A third cause, one that is rather painful to contemplate, is what Simon Johnson, former chief economist at the IMF and now at MIT, calls *capture*: a specific elite gains control of policy making and implementation.[14] Finance captured politicians—to some extent with its ever-increasing money, and to some extent by staffing the key executive branch positions, such as Treasury, with its own people. But that was only secondary. The primary factor was by dominating the policy and ideological space with elegant and untried economic theories about efficient markets and deregulation. The fast-prosperity performance of a finance-led economy in the initial age of Robert

Rubin cemented finance's position (while hugely filling its coffers and appetites).

One of us doesn't quite buy this argument; the other doesn't enjoy it, but won't let us drop it. One of us points out that financial interests had always found doors in Washington open to them since the days of, well, Alexander Hamilton. The other points to a qualitative shift between an FDR who would appoint a Joe Kennedy to run the SEC precisely because he had been a (very wealthy) malefactor who had changed his spots, and more recent appointments justified by the unwarranted assumption that what is good for Wall Street must be good for Main Street too. Either way, both perspectives merit a place in this consideration of what caused America's pro-finance policies.

There is little dispute but that the successive political decisions to loosen the regulation of finance set a vicious cycle in motion. Deregulation of finance did produce the successful innovations of low-cost brokerages (such as Charles Schwab) and low-cost investment funds (such as Vanguard), which offered value, safety, and efficiency—exactly what the deregulators imagined would be the main impact. But in retrospect, they were not the rule but the exception. As each chunk of finance was deregulated, it turned out to be that the newly free-to-compete financial intermediaries were much better at drumming up business by promising their clients that they could beat the market and become rich than at providing value by soberly matching risks to risk-bearing capacity.

There was extraordinary pent-up demand for what Princeton economist Burton Malkiel calls "castles in the air."[15]

And when your principal business model is selling your clients a piece of cloud-cuckoo-land, charging low fees is not an advantage but rather a signal that you do not think the particular cloud you are selling is worth very much. Thus a freer market produced higher fees for many of the biggest financial intermediaries rather than lower fees. And the recipients of those fees looked on the rapid growth of the financial sector, saw that it was good, and promptly set out to lobby for yet more.

Finance and the Sectoral Unbalancing

Thus finance grew: from about 3 percent of the economy at the start of the 1950s to almost 9 percent today. It was the industry of the future for upper, and not-so-upper, middle-class Americans who listened attentively and paid handsomely to the financial professionals who would tell them how to beat the market with their 401(k); for public and private trustees who sought to somehow attain the investment returns they believed they ought to promise clients and beneficiaries; for corporate managers who listened attentively and paid financial professionals handsomely to tell them how undertaking such-and-such an acquisition would unleash enormous synergies; for foreigners seeking safe harbors for their wealth as a form of political risk insurance; and most of all for the financial professionals whose incomes boomed above all measures.

As the proportion of the economy in manufacturing fell from 21 percent to 14 percent, the proportion of the economy in the FIRE—finance, insurance, and real estate—trans-actions rose. The fall of manufacturing is huge. The rise in finance took up most of that—a neat and major reshaping of the economy. Policy created. And nobody told anybody just what new shape and content those policies were giving to our economy.

As Cecchetti and Kharroubi point out, it is not surprising that such a boom in finance not only does not boost but actually retards the growth of the rest of the economy.[16] Remember, finance overwhelmingly provides only intermediary services to the rest of the economy. Nobody eats the advice of M&A strategists. As the source of ultimate value, it is the growth of the nonfinancial economy that in the end is the real economic growth of the economy. Most of finance is simply an *intermediate good*—good only in what other commodities it allows us to produce more of. And so Cecchetti and Kharroubi concluded that "the level of financial development is good only up to a point, after which it becomes a drag on growth, and that a fast-growing financial sector is detrimental." And this is because:

> Financial sector growth benefits disproportionately
> high collateral/low productivity projects . . . the strong
> development in sectors like construction, where returns
> on projects are relatively easy to pledge as collateral but
> productivity (growth) is relatively low . . . Where finan-
> ciers employ the [most] skilled workers . . . productivity
> growth is lower than it would be had . . . entrepreneurs
> attract[ed] the [most] skilled labour . . . [Thus] financial

booms in which skilled labour work for the financial
sector, are sub-optimal when the bargaining power
of financiers is sufficiently large . . . Manufacturing
industries . . . that are in competition for resources with
finance are particularly damaged by financial booms . . .
manufacturing sectors that are either R&D-intensive
or dependent on external finance suffer disproportionate reductions in productivity growth when finance
booms . . .[17]

Joshua Aizenman et al. concur, writing of a "financial
Dutch disease."[18] What were the useful end products produced by the hypertrophied growth and frenzied innovation
of finance? Was capital in the 2000s better allocated across sectors and firms than in the 1950s, thus accelerating economic
growth? Were risks better hedged and distributed? Were corporate managers on average more competent and more aligned
in their interests with stakeholders? Was the job of the Federal
Reserve at managing the macroeconomy made easier? To ask
these questions is enough. The answer is, in each case, no.

How It Happened: The Deregulatory Impulse

The deregulatory impulse was not a one-off, once-and-for-
all sudden change in policy. As Berkeley's Barry Eichengreen
writes, it was rather that "the banking rules . . . died by a
thousand small cuts." Although the keystone of the Great
Depression–era regulatory structure was repealed in 1999
and although that did enable additional risk-taking and thus

systemic risk generation and additional growth in the financial sector, it was merely the end point of a very long process. Eichengreen traces the start to 1980 and the abolition of the Federal Reserve's ceiling on interest rates on bank deposits, Regulation Q. But it actually started before, in the 1970s.[19] It was in 1970 that investment banks had first been allowed to publicly list their equity shares, thus beginning the process of turning investment banks from partnerships where every desk was a risk-management department of its own to our current system in which every single major investment and commercial bank in New York was bankrupt at the end of 2008 but for government rescue.

Why? Because, starting in the 1970s, we got not pragmatism but ideology, often wrapped in abstract theory, in our management and regulation of the financial sector. We got not a financial regulatory system that nudged in the direction of societal well-being, but rather one that put the ideological deregulatory interest above all.

Government thus once again reshaped the economy by opening a new economic space, this time by dismantling the complex structures first erected in the New Deal that had tamed and regulated finance. As in past redesigns, market forces promptly surged through the opened floodgates. A burst of entrepreneurial innovation once again drove the rapid growth of a new leading sector, a sector that ramified throughout the economy and, as in past redesigns, creating—along with new jobs, ideas, and riches—a more powerful, we would say now dominant, political interest. But this time the design was not concrete: nobody set out an image of what we would get. What we got was finance.

Deregulation as an American political movement got its start when Alfred Kahn in the Carter administration headed a group of technocrats who asserted—correctly—that government regulation of transportation had become highly dysfunctional. In transportation, the regulatory framework set up by the Federal Aviation Administration essentially prohibited airlines from competing on price. They competed on quality instead. Business travelers whose firms paid for their tickets were happy. The firms for which they traveled were less so. And those seeking rapid, cheap, cattle-car-like transportation from city to city or from city to vacation spot and back found themselves largely priced out of the market. Passenger air travel deregulation—Kahn's first, signature initiative and the one that got him promoted to greater influence within the Carter administration—was popular among Washington technocrats and very popular indeed among middle-class, would-be vacation travelers.

Alfred Kahn then spearheaded a movement to extend deregulation to land transport.

The Interstate Commerce Commission got its start as an agency to protect farmers from being gouged by the monopoly railroads that served their areas. It soon found itself protecting railroads from the unpleasant realities of competition. In an industry with as high a proportion of fixed to variable costs and as durable a capital stock as railroads, the free-market equilibrium oscillates between three states: monopoly routes in which prices soar and railroads charge what the traffic will bear; competitive routes along which there is excess capacity at prices that cover costs, in which price thus drops to marginal cost, and in which railroads lose money hand over fist; and competitive routes along which capacity building has not kept pace with high-value demand, in which prices soar, and railroads make money hand over fist. Such a market structure is nerve-racking for railroads and their owners—both incumbents and potential entrants. It is also nerve-racking for customers, who are never sure what the future probabilities of the three states are and thus cannot plan either for a world in which rail transport will be cheap or for one in which rail transport will be expensive. Thus the ICC could make everybody happy by making rail charges predictable (if high) and guaranteeing profits for railroads—until trucking appeared on the new interstate highway system.

Trucking promised to undercut ICC-mandated railroad pricing for many types of goods and routes. The ICC thus extended its mandate to the regulation of trucking charges. The International Brotherhood of Teamsters applauded, used its political muscle to back the ICC, and grew to be two million strong. Joint deregulation of railroads and trucking seemed to be—was—a good-government move pleasing to everybody save the Teamsters' union. But Teamster endorsements of Nixon and Reagan did not win them any influence within the Republican policy caucus, and a union that had moved out of the Democratic Party column had little political leverage over Carter's technocrats.

The deregulation movement shifted to energy. The interaction of the Nixon administration's wage and price controls, the tripling of world oil prices as a result of the Arab oil embargo imposed on the West after the 1973 Yom Kippur Egyptian and Syrian attack on Israel, the consequent recognition by Saudi Arabia of exactly how much market power it possessed as the swing producer, the legacy regulatory framework of the Texas Railroad Commission, and the ad hoc and confused Ford and Carter administration reactions to the additional temporary tripling of world oil prices as a result of the Iranian Revolution all left the United States with old oil, new oil, controlled oil, uncontrolled oil—and occasional gasoline shortages and gas lines. Removing this irrational and counterproductive framework was a major Reagan administration win—both in policy and political terms. Energy deregulation reached a kind of monitory crisis in the California electricity deregulation, and the crisis the most successful gamers of that deregulated market triggered. The early energy deregulation was followed up by moves to deregulate telecommunications: to break up AT&T and to let Judge Greene (who presided over the breakup of the AT&T monopoly) and God sort it out.

How It Happened: Financial Deregulation

Even before Alfred Kahn's efforts, there was pressure for financial deregulation. Constant worries about the inequities created by a scattershot system of employer-sponsored pensions and the limited income replacement rates offered by Social Security led to a search for policies that might provide Americans with incentives to save more for retirement and might at the same time substantially help both corporate America and Wall Street. In 1978 Louisiana senator Russell

Long's Finance Committee inserted a provision into the IRS code allowing the deferral of taxes on deferred income until that income was realized. And so the 401(k)—the individual retirement account—was born. Corporate America saw this as an opportunity to shift market risk off its back and books and transfer it to its employees; defined benefit pensions began to be terminated one after the other and replaced by IRA contributions. The number of IRA accounts exploded—a gigantic boon to Wall Street.

For one thing, the replacement of the pension plan by the 401(k) propelled the lucrative business of helping individuals figure out how and where to invest their 401(k) money, and provided an ever-giving gift of custodial and management fees. Fees of 2 percent per year, year after year, for accounts that would sit for thirty years were not uncommon, and they ate a hefty part of the nest egg—not to mention all those additional fees and kickbacks from investment funds to brokers and managers who were compensated not so much when their clients made money as when their clients' portfolios churned. Second, it fueled a lowbrow financial-press and TV industry: a great many more people now had skin in the game on Wall Street and thought they needed to follow it. Third, it funded those willing to make markets, provide liquidity, and be smart money—to buy when the guests on *Mad Money* said "Sell!" and sell when those guests said "Buy!"

In the 1970s, rising inflation made Regulation Q restrictions on the nominal interest rates commercial banks could pay on deposits ever more burdensome. Savers sought alternatives that would not fall as far behind increasing inflation, and money flowed out of the banks that were prohibited from raising interest rates to compete. And so both savers and banks lobbied to have Congress abrogate Regulation Q. Nobody was lobbying for a continuation of interest rate ceilings.

As early as 1974, under Nixon, Congress allowed banks in New Hampshire and Massachusetts to pay interest on negotiable order of withdrawal (NOW) checking accounts. It then extended that privilege to the rest of New England in 1976. And with deregulation of transportation a substantial policy and political success, the Democrats in Congress and President Carter found themselves looking around for additional industries in which deregulation would be smart and popular. They settled on finance, and extended interest on checking accounts to the entire nation at the end of 1980. The Depository Institutions Deregulation Act gradually phased out the Federal Reserve's interest rate ceilings, making banks able to again compete for funds via offering higher interest rates.

The repeal of Regulation Q started the ball rolling. In its wake, mortgage-centered S&Ls found themselves under intensified competitive pressure. Before the repeal, they had been empowered to offer higher interest rates than banks on deposits. Facing additional competitive pressure, they cried out to Congress. And Congress heard their cry. The Garn-St. Germain Depository Institutions Act of 1982 allowed S&Ls to enter essentially all branches of the commercial banking business as well as their mortgage niche and keep government insurance on their deposits, and thus able to expand their operations and embark on more risky investment strategies.

Because the Garn-St. Germain Act did not come with additional regulations that limited the risk S&Ls could now take on, it prepared the way for the late 1980s savings and loan financial crisis. Thrift institutions had been empowered to take on additional risk. They had been subject to no additional regulatory restraint. And they reacted as one might expect.

The elementary economics of moral hazard and deposit insurance tells us that such a situation is potentially dangerous and calls not for a relaxation but for an intensification of regulatory supervision over the assets and portfolios held by banks. Banks subject to interest rate ceilings can park their assets in long-term government, mortgage, and high-grade corporate bonds and compete to widen their scale of operations by improving service and increase their margins by cutting costs. There is no great percentage for them in raising the riskiness of their portfolios—hedge fund–style asset management is not their area of competitive expertise; running an efficient and friendly retail banking operation is. But once banks can compete on interest rates, the game changes: the heads-we-win, tails-the-government-pays game of risky portfolios becomes an attractive one for financial institutions to play. Indeed, it becomes a necessary one, for those that don't play would see their deposits flow out. More aggressive regulatory supervision and more individualized examination is thus a necessary concomitant of interest rate deregulation.

As commercial banks in turn found themselves under competitive pressure from thrifts, they sought regulatory relief themselves. Headed by Bankers Trust, they went not to lobby Congress but to lobby the Federal Reserve. In December 1986, the Fed very creatively interpreted Glass-Steagall to allow commercial banks to underwrite mortgage-backed securities, commercial bonds, and other investment banking activities as long as such activities were limited to less than one-twentieth of their total revenues. That allowable fraction grew over time. In a very rare overruling of its chief, Paul Volcker, the Federal Reserve Board authorized commercial banks to further expand their investment banking–related activities. Under Volcker's successor, Alan Greenspan, the one-twentieth limit on revenue from investment banking grew to one-quarter.

Restrictions on bond quality effectively reserved the bond market for companies that were already quite solid. Lesser firms and lesser investment banks, along with the major investment banks, argued that they should be allowed to issue *junk bonds*—bonds that had a very high yield not because they had been issued as investment grade and then seen the fortunes of the company deteriorate, but bonds that were a riverboat gamble from the very beginning. Local bank lobbyists—especially for S&Ls—argued that modern tools of portfolio management made restrictions on what banks, especially savings and loan associations, could hold in their portfolios outmoded and in need of relaxation.

As the 1980s rolled into its second half, oil prices collapsed, and the oil patch went bust, a great many of the S&Ls on the southern prairie found themselves under water. Their response was to "gamble for resurrection"—to use their government insurance guarantee to hold onto deposits as they invested in riskier and riskier and, they hoped, higher-return portfolios.[20] Initially, regulators objected. But the deregulatory camp's response was twofold: on the intellectual level, it was the S&Ls' money, and they were adults and should be allowed to gamble with it; on the political level, campaign contributions spoke louder than the regulators who pointed out that as the S&L's went under, it was no longer theirs but rather the government's and the taxpayers' money they were gambling with.

When financial institution regulators objected to what S&Ls were doing even under newer, laxer regulatory frameworks, the savings and loan industry summoned its congressmen and senators. The most famous of those blocking attempts to keep financial institutions from gambling for resurrection with government-guaranteed money—attempts to keep savings and loans from playing "heads we win, tails the taxpayer loses"—were the Senate's "Keating Five": Alan Cranston (D-CA), Dennis DeConcini (D-AZ), John Glenn (D-OH), John McCain (R-AZ), and Donald W. Riegle Jr. (D-MI). The consequence was the savings and loan crisis of the early 1990s, a $300 billion lost-deposit bill to the taxpayer, and the creation of the Resolution Trust Corporation to resolve the situation. As about half the failed S&Ls were in Texas, this was a rich case of the rest of the United States giving Texas not a loan but a gift of over $100 billion, something the Greeks now wish the Eurozone had done.

The 1970s had seen investment banks allowed to publicly list their equity shares. And in the 1990s, these banks took advantage to engage in a merger wave to generate not economy of scale within, but economies of scope outside their investment banking niches. Bankers Trust was a trust house.

Alex. Brown & Sons was a brokerage business. They merged. Others merged as well. And commercial banks began lobbying harder as the deregulation lobbying arms race between the branches of the financial services industry intensified.

The final stage, the repeal of Glass-Steagall, was set in motion in 1998. Sandy Weill's Travelers Insurance Group convinced John Reed's Citicorp that they should merge in spite of the Glass-Steagall requirement that the merged entity sell off all of Travelers' insurance business, betting that they could get Glass-Steagall repealed before it applied to their new Citigroup.

The Federal Reserve, Congress, and the Treasury all looked on this with enthusiasm. The profits of the investment banking oligarchy appeared far in excess of what any competitive market ought to deliver. The investment banks had, it seemed, a unique ability to maneuver through thickets of regulations. And the equity return premium's rewards to those with deep pockets and the patience to take on real estate, equity, derivative, and other risks reaped outsize returns indicated that financial markets were doing badly at mobilizing society's risk-bearing capacity. These suggested to the Federal Reserve and the Treasury that institutional experimentation was in order. More competition for investment-banking oligarchs from commercial bankers and insurance companies with deep pockets seemed likely to reduce the investment banking industry's unconscionable profits and improve the flow of capital through the economy. The technocratic arguments that Reed and Weill deployed had powerful influence on the Federal Reserve and the Treasury.

The growth of modern technical mathematical finance was an arrow in the deregulators' quiver. Old-fashioned notions of what constituted a safe portfolio and a safe asset were outmoded, people said. The new financial math of options, derivatives, hedges, and diffusion processes allowed much more sophisticated, subtle, and effective forms of risk management—as long as they were deployed by financial professionals furnished with enough computers and paid highly enough. The fact that this new system of modern finance delivered a 25 percent collapse in the stock market on one single day in October 1987 should have given regulators and academics considerable pause. It did not.

And financial services lobbyists were always welcome on Capitol Hill, where members had learned that deregulation— even when, as in the S&L crisis, it went horribly wrong—was not punished by voters and was accompanied by the ample topping-off of political campaign war chests and lucrative careers after public service.

One would think that the reaction to the S&L crash of the early 1990s would have been that financial deregulation had gone too far. But it was not to be so. Even with bank bust and the $300 billion—5 percent of a year's GDP—bill that the government had just paid, financial deregulatory pressure continued to build.[21] The memory of the great financial collapse and the Great Depression among those trading in financial markets was fading. Policy makers' belief that modern tools of macroeconomic management had made a repetition of the Great Depression impossible was widespread and growing. And so the S&L crisis did not reverse deregulatory momentum.

Glass-Steagall's repeal by the Gramm-Leach-Bliley Act of 1999 was thus the end point of a more than quarter-century-long process of financial deregulation. For decades, commercial banks and shadow banks had been allowed to carry out broader and broader ranges of activities with little or no expansion of oversight in any form.

How It Happened: Financial Crises and the Fading Memory of the Great Depression

Among bankers and other portfolio managers, the straitjackets on the riskiness of portfolios and on the pooling of capital from different sources were not seen as constraints as long as those at the top of organizations had lived through the Great Depression as adults in their industry. The memory wasn't of institutional franchises that had vanished in the 1930s and so destroyed a great deal of future profit-making potential simply because they were overleveraged. Nobody sought to repeat that. Risk the entire future stream of profits from your enterprise in order to squeeze out a few more percentage points this year from a riskier portfolio? Not a strategy that made sense.

Among policymakers, the principal reason for the tight controls on risk present in the New Deal's regulatory apparatus was the fear that another great stock market crash and banking bust would produce another Great Depression unless financiers were required to hold much safer portfolios than such gunslingers would if they were left to their own devices. This credit channel externality meant that the regulated competitive financial markets could not do the job of providing underpinnings for macroeconomic stability and should not be asked to do so. But by the 1970s, absent the nominal anchor provided by the gold standard, it was savers' wealth threatened by inflation rather than leveraged entrepreneurs' enterprises threatened by deflation that was seen as the danger. Requiring low-risk, low return portfolios did guard against deflationary catastrophe but left savers vulnerable to an inflationary one.

Moreover, the intellectual victory of Milton Friedman and Anna Jacobson Schwartz's *Monetary History of the United States* in economic history and the broader intellectual victory of Milton Friedman and his brand of monetarism in both macroeconomic theory and central banking policy made the tight regulatory control of financial market portfolios an unnecessary set of suspenders.[22] The Federal Reserve could prevent deflation simply by properly managing the money stock. The causal chain that had led to the Great Depression would thus be interrupted at its origin, and did not require interventions that degraded the credit channel's ability to finance enterprise.

What had been seen as firebreaks against panic, contagion, bankruptcy, crash, and depression became seen as blockages to the flow of capital to people outside of the tie- and suit-wearing power structure. Junk bonds, subprime mortgages, securitization to pool and diversify risk, and the construction of financial derivatives to carve up and distribute risks (and thus provide vehicles for savers seeking safety to commit their funds to nontraditional borrowers who were not themselves assured of already possessing that safety)—these were all seen as ways of broadening access to capital, potentially democratizing finance, and boosting upward mobility, not to mention boosting financial firms. And it wasn't seen as just a Republican money-grabbing plot. After all, the overwhelmingly Democratic Congressional Black Caucus were big boosters of subprime borrowing. The restriction of the mortgage market to those who qualified for conforming loans was, in their eyes, discriminatory in effect if not in intent.

A pragmatic approach to high finance would have seen it as an important sector that needed to be regulated delicately, because it has a built-in tendency to run amok and in doing so causing far-flung economic destruction. Finance needs to accomplish its proper missions. Transactions, patterns, and practices that advance those missions properly should be made easy and cheap. It needs to be dissuaded from its improper functions. Those forms of finance should be burdensome, laborious, and costly. That is not what we got.

If we look back—way back, across the past two centuries— this is what we see: speculative manias followed by panics, crashes, and steep recessions: 1837, 1873, 1893, 1907.

The most prominent was, of course, the 1929 crash that triggered the Great Depression. The American policy response to 1929 was strong financial regulation, and we had no manias, panics or crashes for two full generations. We then deliberately set about dismantling that regulatory framework. A flurry of innovation-propelled financialization and the very rapid growth of finance as a sector, substantially offsetting, in terms of the composition of GDP, the simultaneous hollowing out of American industry while at the same time abetting it. Deliberately, but not concretely—instead, driven by ideology and often expressed in terms of newly coined economic and finance theory—we reshaped the economy. Speculative manias and crashes ensued: in 2000, we escaped serious recession; in 2008, we did not.

We cannot afford to have a high-finance sector so large that we again run risks of another 2008—or, even worse, another 1929. Finance should not be once again our leading growth sector; rather, it should be our leading shrink sector, perhaps replacing manufacturing in that role. And yet we have no plans to cut it back. Quite the contrary. We are right on track to reflate finance, itself now ever more powerful, one could argue—now dominant—politically. To say the very least, this is most unfortunate.

Conclusion

We have been harshly critical of the ideological turn in American economic policy that began in the early 1980s. We have been critical because the speakers, thinkers, and actors who made that turn "knew" things that they did not know and which proved wrong. They "knew"—without looking at the world at all—that the American economy:

- Was hog-tied by excessive regulation everywhere, all of which needed to be pruned back to unleash the private sector,

- Provided insufficient incentives for enterprise and entrepreneurship, which needed larger financial rewards to spur it forward,

    and

- Had fallen victim to an ossified "demosclerosis" in which too many interest groups had acquired claims to income and wealth not derived from success in the market.[1]

Thus the principal task of political economy was to:

- Cut back all forms of government regulation and interference with the marketplace, open the markets so that entrepreneurs would rush in, innovate, grow, and in so doing reinvigorate and reshape the economy.

  and

- That is what happened.

There was no effort whatever to provide a concrete image of how the real economy would be reshaped when it all had been sorted out.

This policy turn has, we believe, been a huge mistake for America: a mistake in how the major economic choices that reshape the economy are made, as well as a misfortune in outcome. For, as John Maynard Keynes wrote in the 1920s:

> The world is not so governed from above that private and social interest always coincide. It is not so managed here below that in practice they coincide. It is not a correct deduction from the principles of economics that enlightened self-interest always operates in the public interest. Nor is it true that self-interest generally is enlightened . . .[2]

High-finance churning and creaming, real estate transacting, and health-care claims processing were not the industries of the future to produce big positive spillovers. But they turned out to be the concrete shape of the economy implanted by Washington policy makers. Busy but useless, empty but still flabby, as a proportion of GDP they largely replaced the great swaths of manufacturing that had been liposuctioned out. Unattractive as they are, they are the new shape of the American economy as wrought by American policy makers. And tilting the distribution of income in favor of the very rich sitting at value-appropriation chokepoints in the economy did not unleash productive waves of entrepreneurship that benefited us all. The communities of engineering practice in industry built up and nurtured since the days of Alexander Hamilton were not all shoddy and outworn garments America should, out of goodwill, be happy to donate to poorer emerging markets.

But our complaint is not that the turn around 1980 was motivated by the wrong ideology.

We do not call for its replacement by a different ideology, one that we "know" without looking at the world at all will benefit the American economy. We do not know in advance that more government regulation is always good, that every manufacturing job is worth keeping, that each proposed piece of infrastructure development is a national blessing, that soak-the-rich is always a win-win policy.

What we do know is that since the days of Hamilton, it is a fact that America's successful economic policy has been pragmatic, not ideological. It has been concrete, not abstract. It has been image-able, not *ex ante* unknowable and indescribable. And it was not unspeakable. Thus we do believe that we know not what to think but rather how to think about economic policy: a distrust of ideology or, as sociologist Daniel Bell might have put it but did not in his hopeful 1950s book *The End of Ideology*, an ideology of non-ideology.[3] Or as Keynes did put it:

> We cannot therefore settle on abstract grounds, but
> must handle on its merits in detail what Burke termed
> "one of the finest problems in legislation," namely, to
> determine what the State ought to take upon itself
> to direct by the public wisdom, and what it ought to
> leave, with as little interference as possible, to individ-
> ual exertion . . . and to do this without Bentham's prior
> presumption that interference is, at the same time, "gen-
> erally needless" and "generally pernicious" . . .[4]

Perhaps the worst damage to our national capacity to think through the issues was the (largely successful) attempt by those who made the policy turn around 1980 to classify America's pragmatic political economy tradition as just another ideology, a counter-ideology to laissez-faire, as ideological Keynesianism. Read Keynes and you find, immediately after his denunciations of laissez-faire and his call to look at questions on the merits, an equally strong denunciation of left-wing ideologies:

> I criticise doctrinaire State Socialism . . . because it
> misses the significance of what is actually happening;
> because it is, in fact, little better than a dusty survival of
> a plan to meet the problems of fifty years ago, based on

a misunderstanding of what someone said a hundred years ago . . .[5]

We need to recover that American tradition of pragmatic engagement with questions of economic policy and equitable growth. It is the case that, since its very beginning, the United States has again and again shifted its economy and pointed it in a new growth direction. These intelligent designs were taken by government, backed by powerful and often broad political forces, and guided by a broadly shared vision of how the economy ought to change. As entrepreneurial energy and activity surged into the new economic space, the economy was invigorated and transformed in unforeseeable ways. These reshapings made America into, as Leon Trotsky called it in his autobiography, "the furnace where the future is being forged." America still has some of that fire, most notably in Silicon Valley. But does anybody really believe that America's most recent redesign opened up to vast and positive growth?

In that latest redesign, beginning in the 1980s, the new direction was—uniquely in American history—selected not pragmatically but ideologically, and presented not concretely but abstractly. Government again signaled the direction; cleared the way; arranged the means. Entrepreneurs rushed in, innovated, took risks, profited, and expanded that new growth direction as all forms of red tape, government regulation, and interference with the marketplace were cut back and the market was left to sort it all out. Controls were dismantled. The economy was redirected and reshaped. But it was not reinvigorated. Not much was added to general prosperity.

Norms were broken as the domain of market forces and market logic was expanded so that social structures were subordinated and corroded by market forces. Their replacements are, when available, difficult and costly. And it did not benefit American power in the world nor the balance of power within America. It is extremely unlikely that America would have chosen that redesign were it to have been presented concretely instead of abstractly and ideologically.

So what should we do now?

America needs another economic redesign.

We do not propose the content of such a redesign, complete with dubious numerical targets. That is not how it happened in the successful American past. New directions were not the bright ideas of clever economists or blue-ribbon commissions. It is not the way for today.

But we do have a bright idea that we think consummately important. We propose one change—a change that is simple to understand but likely to prove difficult to implement.

That single change is: Shift discussion of economic policy to the concrete, where it had recurrent successes. Pull it out from the speculative realms of ideology and its handmaiden theoretical abstractions. Push thinking and talking and proposing about what we should do about our economy into concrete terms. Insist that proposed shifts be couched so as to be image-able, as in, "This is the kind of thing we will get."

This will help more than anything else we can imagine to reshape the economy in a positive direction, and our society as well.

Notes

Introduction

1. Data from the Federal Reserve Bank of St. Louis's FRED—Federal Reserve Economic Data—website: https://research.stlouisfed.org/fred2/; https://research.stlouisfed.org/fred2/graph/?id=VAPGDPMA.

2. The economist who has done the most to count and track the hypertrophy of the American finance sector is New York University's Thomas Philippon. His CV is at http://pages.stern.nyu.edu/~tphilipp/vita.pdf. See especially: "Finance vs. Wal-Mart: Why Are Financial Services so Expensive?" in *Rethinking the Financial Crisis*, edited by Alan Blinder, Andrew Lo, and Robert Solow (New York: Russell Sage Foundation, 2013); "Wages and Human Capital in the U.S. Financial Industry: 1909–2006," with Ariell Reshef, *Quarterly Journal of Economics*, May 2012; "An International Look at the Growth of Modern Finance" with Ariell Reshef, *Journal of Economic Perspectives* 27, no. 2 (Spring 2013); and "Has the U.S. Finance Industry Become Less Efficient?" *American Economic Review* 105, no. 4 (April 2015).

3. Ralph E. Gomory and William J. Baumol make this important argument with more than the requisite mathematical rigor in *Global Trade and Conflicting National Interests* (Cambridge, MA: MIT Press, 2001). See also Paul A. Samuelson, "Where Ricardo and Mill Rebut and Confirm Arguments of Mainstream Economists Supporting Globalization," *Journal of Economic Perspectives* 18, no. 3 (Summer 2004): 135–146.

4. Warren Buffett called derivatives "financial weapons of mass destruction" in his 2002 annual report to Berkshire Hathaway shareholders.

5. Philippon and Reshef, "Wages and Human Capital in the U.S. Financial Industry: 1909–2006."

Chapter 1

1. See, for example, James Madison, "Speech in Congress Opposing the National Bank on February 2, 1791," *Constitution Society*, http://www.constitution.org/jm/17910202_bank.htm: "it was not possible to discover in [the Constitution] the power to incorporate a [National] Bank. . . . No argument could be drawn from the terms "common defence, and general welfare." The power as to these general purposes, was limited to acts laying taxes for them; and the general purposes themselves were limited and explained by the particular enumeration subjoined . . ."

2. *Letters and Other Writings of James Madison*, Vol 3, 1816–1828. (New York: R. Worthington, 1884), 542.

3. Laura Ingalls Wilder, *The Long Winter* (New York: Harper & Row: 1953).

4. John Robert Seeley, *The Expansion of England* first published 1883 (New York: Cosimo Classics History, 2005), 8.

5. John Brewer, *The Sinews of Power: War, Money and the English State, 1688–1783* (New York: Alfred A. Knopf, 1988).

6. Adam Smith, *An Inquiry into the Nature and Causes of the Wealth of Nations* (London, 1776), Book IV, Chapter 7, Part II, http://www.gutenberg.org/files/3300/3300-h/3300-h.

7. Alexander Hamilton, *Report to the House of Representatives on Manufactures* (Washington: U.S. Treasury, 1791), http://www.constitution.org/ah/rpt_manufactures.pdf.

8. W. Arthur Lewis, *Evolution of the International Economic Order* (Princeton, NJ: Princeton University Press, 1978).

9. Alexander Hamilton, Letter to Robert Morris of April 30, 1781, http://founders.archives.gov/documents/Hamilton/01-02-02-1167.

10. They do not have one in the offing in large part because of the dominance within Europe of Germany, and the fact that due to Germany's export orientation depression elsewhere in Europe produces a weaker currency and thus a more prosperous Germany.

11. Paul Bairoch, *Economics and World History: Myths and Paradoxes* (Chicago: University of Chicago Press, 1993), 33, table 3.1.

Notes

12. Indeed, the adverse monetary shocks administered in the course of his political war on the Second Bank of the United States may have generated the largest business-cycle recession America was to experience before the failure of Jay Cooke & Co. sparked the Panic of 1873.

Chapter 2

1. Eric Foner, *Free Soil, Free Labor, Free Men: The Ideology of the Republican Party before the Civil War* (Oxford: Oxford University Press, 1970).

2. Paul Bairoch, *Economics and World History: Myths and Paradoxes* (Chicago: University of Chicago Press, 1993), table 2.2.

3. Ibid., table 3.3.

4. Leon Trotsky, *My Life* (New York: Charles Scribner, 1930), https://www.marxists.org/ebooks/trotsky/my-life/my-life-trotsky.epub.

5. Abraham Lincoln, *First Annual Message*, December 30, 1861, http://www.presidency.ucsb.edu/ws/?pid=29502.

6. Theodore Roosevelt, "Campaign Speech," October 15, 1896, http://projects.vassar.edu/1896/altgeld.html.

7. Jeff Weintraub, "Rum, Romanism, and Rebellion: Some Historical Reflections on Pastors and Presidential Candidates," *Jeff Weintraub Commentaries and Controversy* blog, March 16, 2008, http://jeffweintraub.blogspot.com/2008/03/rum-romanism-and-rebellion-some.html.

8. Oliver Wendell Holmes, "Dissent in Lochner v. New York" 198 US 45, 1905, http://caselaw.findlaw.com/scripts/getcase.pl?court=US&vol=198&invol=45.

9. Eric Schlosser, "'I Aimed for the Public's Heart, and . . . Hit It in the Stomach': 'The Jungle' Was a Socialist's Cry for Labor Justice. It Launched a Consumer Movement Instead," *Chicago Tribune*, May 21, 2006, http://articles.chicagotribune.com/2006-05-21/features/0605210414_1_upton-sinclair-trust-free.

10. "Prosperity" quotation is commonly (though wrongly) attributed to Herbert Hoover.

11. Franklin Delano Roosevelt, *First Inaugural Address*, March 4, 1933, http://www.c-span.org/video/?5792-1/president-franklin-d-roosevelt-inaugural-address.

12. Kenneth Jackson, *Crabgrass Frontier* (New York: Oxford University Press, 1985), 196.

Chapter 3

1. Daniel Bell (1962), *The End of Ideology* (Cambridge, MA: Harvard University Press, 1962).

2. http://web.archive.org/web/20051124190902/http://www .eisenhowermemorial.org/presidential-papers/first-term/ documents/1147.cfm.

3. White House Office of Management and Budget historical tables, "Summary of Receipts, Outlays, and Surpluses or Deficits (-) as Percentages of GDP: 1930–2020," table 1.2, https://www.whitehouse .gov/omb/budget/Historicals.

4. Emmanuel Saez, "Striking It Richer: The Evolution of Top Incomes in the United States (Updated with 2012 preliminary estimates," September 3, 2013, http://eml.berkeley.edu//~saez/ saez-UStopincomes-2012.pdf.

5. Lawrence Mishel and Alyssa Davis, "Top CEOs Make 300 Time More Than Typical Workers," *Economic Policy Institute,* June 21, 2015, http:// www.epi.org/publication/top-ceos-make-300-times-more-than-workers-pay -growth-surpasses-market-gains-and-the-rest-of-the-0-1-percent/.

6. Kenneth Jackson, *Crabgrass Frontier* (New York: Oxford University Press, 1985), 193, 204, 193. The following paragraphs draw heavily on Jackson's book, then—and to our knowledge still—the best history of America's suburbs.

7. Ibid., 194.

8. Ibid., 196.

9. Ibid., 326.

10. Ibid., 283.

11. James P. Womack, Daniel T. Jones, and Daniel Roos. *The Machine That Changed the World.* (New York: Free Press, 1990, 2007).

12. Jackson, *Crabgrass Frontier*, 241.

13. Michael Carliner, "Development of Federal Homeownership 'Policy,'" *Housing Policy Debate* 9, no. 2 (1998): 299–321.

14. White House Office of Management and Budget historical tables, https://www.whitehouse.gov/omb/budget/Historicals, table 14.5.

15. Robert S. Norris and Hans M. Kristensen, "Global Nuclear Weapons Inventories," *Bulletin of the Atomic Scientists* 66, no. 4 (July 2010): 77–82, table 2.

16. Famous as the policy Trotsky advocated the newly-installed Bolshevik government follow vis-à-vis Imperial Germany and its army in Russia after its successful coup and before its signing of the Peace of Brest-Litovsk. See Tony Cliff, *Trotsky: Sword of the Revolution* (London: Bookmarks, 1990).

17. White House Office of Management and Budget historical tables, https://www.whitehouse.gov/omb/budget/Historicals, table 1.2.

18. G. Andrew Bernat, Jr., "Convergence in State Per Capita Personal Income, 1950–99," *Survey of Current Business* 81, no. 6 (June 2001): 36–48.

19. See Steven Solomon, *Water: The Epic Struggle for Wealth, Power, and Civilization* (New York: HarperCollins, 2010), 325–349.

20. Dwight D. Eisenhower, "Farewell Radio and Television Address to the American People," January 17, 1961, http://www.eisenhower.archives.gov/all_about_ike/speeches/farewell_address.pdf.

21. OECD, *Exchange Control Policy (Centre for Cooperation with the European Economies in Transition)* (Geneva: OECD, 1993), 28.

22. John Gertner's *The Idea Factory: Bell Labs and the Great Age of American Innovation* (London: Penguin Press, 2012) is a very accessible history of Bell Labs' role in innovation in our period and earlier. Bell is no longer anything like its pre-breakup self; indeed, it was bought by the French telecom company Alcatel.

23. Vernon W. Ruttan, *Is War Necessary for Economic Growth? Military Procurement and Technology Development* (New York: Oxford University Press, 2006), 75–77; John A. Alic et al., *Beyond Spinoff: Military and Commercial Technologies in a Changing World* (Boston: Harvard Business School, 1992), 69.

24. Lewis Strauss, speech to the National Association of Science Writers, 1954.

25. Dwight D. Eisenhower, "Atoms for Peace," speech to the UN General Assembly, New York, December 8, 1953.

26. Ruttan, *Is War Necessary for Economic Growth*, 55–57; Alic et al., *Beyond Spinoff*, 60.

27. See Almarin Philips, *Technology and Market Structure: A Study of the Aircraft Industry* (Lexington, MA: Heath Lexington Books, 1971), 32.

28. Alic et al., *Beyond Spinoff*, 60.

29. This may now be changing. See Ben Thompson, "Venture Capital and the Internet's Impact," *Stratechery* (October 14, 2015), https://stratechery.com/2015/venture-capital-and-the-internets-impact/: "Because a company pays for AWS resources as they use them, it is possible to create an entirely new app for basically $0 in your spare time. Or, alternately, if you want to make a real go of it, a founder's only costs are his or her forgone salary and the cost of hiring whomever he or she deems necessary to get a minimum viable product out the door. In dollar terms that means the cost of building a new idea has plummeted from the millions to the (low) hundreds of thousands . . ."

30. Jay Stowsky, "Competing with the Pentagon," *World Policy Journal* 3, no. 4 (Fall 1986): 697–721.

31. US Federal Trade Commission, Bureau of Economics, *Staff Report on the Semiconductor Industry,* January 1977, p. 97. See also Jay Stowsky, *Beating Our Ploughshares into Double-Edged Swords: The Impact of Pentagon Policies on the Commercialization of Advanced Technologies*, BRIE Working Paper 17, presented at Berkeley Roundtable on the International Economy, University of California, Berkeley, April 1986.

32. National Research Council, *Funding a Revolution: Government Support for Computing* (Washington, DC: National Academies Press, 1999), 148.

33. Ibid, 86.

34. MIT Lincoln Labs, "The SAGE Air Defense System," https://www.ll.mit.edu/about/History/SAGEairdefensesystem.html.

35. David C. Mowery, "The Computer Software Industry," in *Sources of Industrial Leadership: Studies in Seven Industries*, ed. David C. Mowery and Richard R. Nelson (New York: Cambridge University Press, 1999).

36. Proxmire issued his famous "Golden Fleece Awards" to projects he viewed as a waste of taxpayer dollars.

37. National Science Foundation, "The Launch of NSFNET," *America's Investment in the Future*, https://www.nsf.gov/about/history/nsf0050/internet/launch.htm.

38. Mariana Mazzucato, *The Entrepreneurial State: Debunking Public vs. Private Sector Myths* (London: Anthem Press, 2013), chapter 5.

39. Ibid., 64–67.

Chapter 4

1. Martin Wolf, personal communication with the authors, October 11, 2015. "And," he went on to say, "it is America that is now ruled by a cabal that has forgotten all about the *developmental state*."

2. See James Fallows (1994), *Looking at the Sun: The Rise of the New East Asian Economic and Political System* (New York: Vintage, 1994). Although two decades old, this is still the best introduction to the long sweep of the history of this development model outside the United States—not that we agree with everything in the book, but very few books two decades old about the world's economy today can still be read with such profit.

3. The classic statement within the field of economic development of these ideas is, Albert Hirschman, *The Strategy of Economic Development* (New Haven, CT: Yale University Press: 1958).

4. J. Bradford DeLong, "Comment on 'Can Domestic Expansionary Policy Succeed in a Globally Integrated Environment?'" in Dean Baker, Gerald Epstein, and Robert Pollin, eds., *Globalization and Progressive Economic Policy* (Cambridge: Cambridge University Press, 1997).

5. The reference point for criticisms of how Hamiltonian developmental-state policies can go horribly wrong is Carlos Diaz-Alejandro (1970), *Essays on the Economic History of the Argentine Republic* (New Haven: Yale Economic Growth Center, 1970). It is another old book—now nearly fifty years old—that can still be read today and teach enormous amounts about its subject.

6. Karl Marx, *Capital: A Critique of Political Economy* vol. I, 1867, https://www.marxists.org/archive/marx/works/1867-c1/p1.htm. The fuller context of the quote is that of dismissing those of his German critics who complain: "But why should we read a book about *England*?": "[If] the German reader shrugs his shoulders . . . I must plainly tell him, 'De te fabula narratur!' Intrinsically, it is not a question of the higher or lower degree of development of the social antagonisms that result from the natural laws of capitalist production.

It is a question of these laws themselves, of these tendencies working with iron necessity towards inevitable results. The country that is more developed industrially only shows, to the less developed, the image of its own future . . ."

7. These questions have been central to virtually the entire career of economist Paul Romer. His website, http://paulromer.net, has become the best place to find deep thinking about what economic theory and the theories of economists have to tell us about growth and innovation.

8. Note that—as China's rapid growth since the fall of Mao Zedong underscores—the East Asian model has nothing in common with the Stalinist model, where as a matter of ideology the economy was kept autarkic, walled off from international markets and world prices—indeed from prices altogether—and the state bureaucratically ran it as one giant conglomerate.

9. As World Bank Research under Lawrence Summers stressed back in 1993 in its report on The East Asian Miracle. See World Bank, *The East Asian Miracle: Economic Growth and Public Policy* (Oxford: Oxford University Press, 1993).

10. Dale Jorgensen and Koji Nomura, "The Industry Origins of the U.S.-Japan Productivity Gap," *Economic Systems Research* 19, no. 3 (2007): 315–412.

11. See John Tang, "Fukoko Kyohei: Evaluating the Impact of Public Investment in Meiji Japan" (Canberra: Australian National University, 2011). "Fukoko Kyohei" was the guiding principle for the Japanese government of the Meiji Restoration. It replaced "revere the emperor and expel the barbarians."

12. At least one of us finds the "generation-long Keynesian slump" interpretation that has been pushed by Paul Krugman since the late-1990s attractive, but suspects that attraction is more because of theoretical intellectual allegiances than rational judgment or knowledge. See Paul Krugman (1998), "It's Baaaack: Japan's Slump and the Return of the Liquidity Trap," *Brookings Papers on Economic Activity* 2 (1998): 137–205.

13. Data on sectoral trade from *OECD Trade by Commodities*, 1990, 1991, and 1992.

14. A point stressed back in the mid-1990s by Paul Krugman. See Paul Krugman, *Exchange Rate Instability* (Cambridge: MIT Press: 1998).

15. Commissariat General du Plan, *Rapport sur les Investissements Internationaux*, April 1992.

16. Michael Gerlach, "Keiretsu Organization in the Japanese Economy," *Politics and Productivity: How Japan's Development Strategy Works*, ed. Chalmers Johnson, Laura D'Andrea Tyson, and John Zysman (New York: HarperBusiness, 1989), chapter 4.

17. OECD, *Economic Outlook* no. 40, December 1986.

18. Paul Krugman, "Is Free Trade Passé?" *Journal of Economic Perspectives* 1, no. 2 (Fall 1987): 131–144.

19. Marcus Tullius Cicero to Titus Pomponius Atticus. See Eric Gruen, *The Last Generation of the Roman Republic* (Berkeley: University of California Press, 1995).

20. Krugman, "Is Free Trade Passé?"

21. According to the International Monetary Fund, growth was 36 percent in 1990; 42 percent in 1995; 42 percent in 2005; and 48.4 percent in 2011. See world-economic-outlook.findthedata.com/.

22. Angus Maddison, *Chinese Economic Performance in the Long Run* (Paris: OECD Development Center, 1998), table 3.13. For an analysis of China's step-by-step groping toward reform and the dual-track pricing, Barry Naughton's *Growing Out of the Plan: Chinese Economic Reform, 1978–1993* (Cambridge: Cambridge University Press, 1995) is one of the first and best.

23. Robert Koopman, Zhi Wang, Shang-Jin Wei ("How Much of Chinese Exports Is Really Made in China? Assessing Domestic Value-Added When Processing Trade Is Pervasive," NBER Working Paper no. 14109 [Washington, DC: National Bureau of Economic Research, June 2008]) estimate that the Chinese share of Chinese exports has increased to about 60 percent. Hiau Looi Kee and Heiwai Tang, ("Domestic Value Added in Chinese Exports," World Bank External Seminars, December 2011) put the figure at 62 percent by 2006, increased from 50 percent in 2000. Robert C. Johnson and Guillermo Noguera, in a later effort ("The Value-Added Content of Trade," *VOX, CEPR's Policy Portal*, June 7, 2011, http://www.voxeu.org/article/value-added-content-trade-new-insights-us-china-imbalance), using, of course, a different methodology, estimate Chinese value added for Chinese manufacturing exports at 40 percent; interestingly their estimate for US manufacturing exports is 49 percent and 47 percent for Germany; their final version of this study ("Accounting for

Intermediates: Production Sharing and Trade in Value Added," *Journal of International Economics* 86, no. 2 [March 2012]: 224–236) states, at the very front, that they find the US-China trade deficit should be reduced by "30–40 per cent" for trade by value added.

24. Overall Chinese value-added to high tech exports is now estimated at 15%: Edward C. Prescott, Ellen R. McGrattan, and Thomas J. Holmes, in "Technology Capital Transfer," Working Paper 687 (Minneapolis, MN: Federal Reserve Bank of Minneapolis, revised November 3, 2011), report that overall Chinese value added to high-tech exports is now estimated at 15 percent; this same source estimates US value added of US high high-tech exports at 30 percent.

25. Alan MacPherson and David Pritchard, "The International Decentralisation of US Commercial Aircraft Production: Implications for US Employment and Trade," *Futures* 35, no. 3 (April 2003): 221–238.

26. OECD, Trade in Value Added Data Base.

27. Wayne M. Morrison places that share at just over 50 percent (*China's Economic Conditions*, Congressional Research Service Report 7-5700, June 26, 2012, figure 6); *China Daily*, June 30, 2006, reports that 70 percent of China's top two hundred exporting firms were foreign invested firms.

28. On Chinese appropriation of high-speed train technology see Jamil Anderlini and Mure Dickie, "China: A Future on Track," *Financial Times*, September 23, 2010. On technology transfer more generally, see US International Trade Commission, *China: Intellectual Property Infringement, Indigenous Innovation Policies, and Frameworks for Measuring the Effects on the U.S. Economy*, USITC Publication #4199, 2010, http://www.usitc.gov/publications/332/pub4199.pdf; also see Prescott, McGrattan, and Holmes, "Technology Capital Transfer." A curious statistic is to be found in the 2010 *China Statistical Yearbook on Science and Technology*, table 5.1 ("China Technology Up-grading"), which lists the growth of in-house expenditures on R&D as growing 25 percent between 2000 and 2009; expenditure on the assimilation of foreign technology at 26 percent, and only 4 percent for expenditure for acquisition of foreign technology. We don't know what to make of these data categories, but the data pique curiosity.

29. On Lowell's New England textiles, see Carol Berkin et al., *Making America: A History of the United States*, vol. 1 (Boston: Wadsworth, 2007), chapter 9 (especially p. 256); on eighteenth-century successful French espionage to learn the secrets of making porcelain, see John Harris, *Industrial Espionage and Technology Transfer: Britain and France in the Eighteenth Century* (Aldershot, UK: Ashgate Press, 1998).

30. Eric Ng, "Overcapacity Plagues Aluminium Sector," *South China Morning Post*, August 19, 2013.

31. Danny Hakim, "Aboard a Cargo Colossus," *New York Times*, October 5, 2014.

32. Ibid. See also Keith Bradsher, "Trade Issues with China Flare Anew," *New York Times*, March 21, 2012.

33. The head of one Chinese producer talked to the American press about his company's success: 95 percent of its production was for export. It got land from the city government at about one-third of the market price. The city government also arranged for low-cost loans from the bank and then, in cooperation with the provincial government, paid most of the interest on those loans. The story is not exceptional; only the free and easy telling of it by the principal actor is. See Bradsher, "Trade Issues with China Flare Anew," and "Solar Tariffs Upheld, but May Not Help in U.S.," *New York Times*, November 8, 2012. The story of Suntech, which blew up on $700 million in dodgy foreign bonds it bought with its oversupply of free capital is to be found in Keith Bradsher, "Suntech, Owing Millions, Faces a Takeover," *New York Times*, March 14, 2013; Clifford Krauss and Keith Bradsher, "China's Global Ambitions, with Loans and Strings Attached," *New York Times*, July 25, 2014; and Diane Cardwell and Keith Bradsher, "Solar Industry Is Rebalanced by U.S. Pressure on China," *New York Times*, July 25, 2014.

34. Michael Pettis merits mention as an early, thorough, and leading exponent of this view; see *Avoiding the Fall: China's Economic Restructuring* (Washington, DC: Carnegie Endowment for International Peace, 2013) and his blog *Michael Pettis' China Financial Markets* (http://blog.mpettis.com/). Guilhem Fabre, *The Lion's Share: What's Behind China's Economic Slowdown*, FMSH-WP-2013, October 2013, https://halshs.archives-ouvertes.fr/halshs-00874077, is very clear and covers in a short space a lot of issues. Quotation from Nicholas

R. Lardy and Nicholas Borst, *A Blueprint for Rebalancing the Chinese Economy*, Policy Brief PB13-02, Peterson Institute for International Economics, http://www.iie.com/publications/pb/pb13-2.pdf.

35. Reuters, 4/4/13. Since 2013 the gap has widened significantly, http://www.reuters.com/article/2013/04/04/economy-mexico-wages-idUSL2N0CR1TY20130404#WR1mLZ417sVA1495.97.

36. Peking University study reported by AFP, July 26, 2014, www.ndtv.com/world-news/china wealth-report-594378.

37. Cited in Lant Pritchett and Lawrence H. Summers, "Growth Slowdowns: Middle-Income Trap vs. Regression to the Mean," *VOX, CEPR's Policy Portal*, December 11, 2014, http://www.voxeu.org/article/growth-slowdowns-middle-income-trap-vs-regression-mean. See also Lant Pritchett and Lawrence H. Summers, "Asiaphoria Meets Regression to the Mean" NBER Working Paper No. 20573, October 2014.

Chapter 5

1. Martin Wolf, "Lunch with the FT: Ben Bernanke," *Financial Times*, October 23, 2015, http://www.ft.com/intl/cms/s/0/0c07ba88-7822-11e5-a95a-27d368e1ddf7.html.

2. Phillippon and Reshef, "An International Look at the Growth of Modern Finance."

3. Dave Kansas and David Weidner, "Volcker Praises the ATM, Blasts Finance Execs, Experts," *Wall Street Journal* (December 8, 2009), http://blogs.wsj.com/marketbeat/2009/12/08/volcker-praises-the-atm-blasts-finance-execs-experts/.

4. "Jack Bogle Explains How the Index Fund Won with Investors," *CNN Money*, July 27, 2015, http://time.com/money/3956351/jack-bogle-index-fund/.

5. See the Uniform Prudential Management of Institutional Funds Act, www.upmifa.org.

6. Thomas Piketty and Gabriel Zucman, "Capital Is Back!: Wealth-to-Income Ratios in Rich Countries, 1700–2010" (Paris: Paris School of Economics, 2013), http://piketty.pse.ens.fr/files/PikettyZucman2013WP.pdf.

7. Neil Irwin, "Wall Street Is Back, Almost as Big as Ever" *New York Times*, May 19, 2015, http://www.nytimes.com/2015/05/19/upshot/wall-street-is-back-almost-as-big-as-ever.html.

8. Robert Manning, testimony to NY State Senate committee on Banks, 16 April, 2007, 10

9. Philippon, "Finance vs. Wal-Mart."

10. George A. Akerlof and Robert J. Shiller, *Phishing for Phools: The Economics of Deception and Manipulation* (Princeton, NJ: Princeton University Press, 2015).

11. Philippon, "Finance vs. Wal-Mart."

12. See L. Randall Wray, *Minsky Crisis* (Annandale-on-Hudson, NY: Bard College, 2011); citing Hyman P. Minsky, *Stabilizing an Unstable Economy* (New Haven, CT: Yale University Press, 1986).

13. Ronald Reagan, Broadcast (August 12, 1986) https://www .youtube.comwatch?v=xhYJS80MgYA&ab_channel=01101010charles.

14. Simon Johnson, "The Quiet Coup," *The Atlantic*, May 2009, http://www.theatlantic.com/magazine/archive/2009/05/ the-quiet-coup/307364/.

15. Burton Malkiel, *A Random Walk Down Wall Street: The Time-Tested Strategy for Successful Investing* (New York: W.W. Norton, 2015).

16. Stephen G. Cecchetti and Enisse Kharroubi, "Why Does Financial Sector Growth Crowd Out Real Economic Growth?" Working Paper no. 490 (Basel: Bank for International Settlements, February 2015), http://www.bis.org/publ/work490.pdf.

17. Ibid.

18. Joshua Aizenman, Yothin Jinjarak, and Donghyun Park, "Financial Development and Output Growth," *VOX, CEPR's Policy Portal*, February 14, 2015, http://www.voxeu.org/article/financial-development -and-output-growth-evidence-east-asia-and-latin-america.

19. Barry Eichengreen, "Financial Crisis: Revisiting the Banking Rules That Died by a Thousand Small Cuts," *Fortune*, January 16, 2015, http://fortune.com/2015/01/16/financial-crisis-bank-regulation/.

20. An analogous process happened in Iceland in 2008. See Friðrik Már Baldursson and Richard Portes, "Gambling for Resurrection in Iceland," January 6, 2014, *VOX, CEPR's Policy Portal*, http://www .voxeu.org/article/gambling-resurrection-iceland.

21. William K Black, *The Best Way to Rob a Bank Is to Own One* (Austin: University of Texas Press, 2005).

22. Milton Friedman and Anna Jacobson Schwartz, *A Monetary History of the United States, 1857–1960* (Princeton, NJ: Princeton University Press, 1971).

Notes

Conclusion

1. See Jonathan Rauch, *Demosclerosis: The Silent Killer of American Government* (New York: Three Rivers Press, 1995).

2. John Maynard Keynes, "The End of Laissez-Faire" (London: Hogarth Press, 1926).

3. Daniel Bell, *The End of Ideology: On the Exhaustion of Political Ideas in the Fifties* (Cambridge, MA: Harvard University Press, 1960).

4. Keynes, "The End of Laissez-Faire.

5. Ibid.

Index

Index

Index

About the Authors

STEPHEN S. COHEN is a professor emeritus and codirector of the Berkeley Roundtable on the International Economy (BRIE) at the University of California, Berkeley, and a visiting scholar at NYU/Wagner.

J. BRADFORD DELONG is a professor of economics at the University of California, Berkeley, a research associate at the National Bureau of Economic Research, a weblogger at the Washington Center for Equitable Growth, and has been a deputy assistant secretary of the US Department of Treasury. He can always be found online at http://bradford-delong.com.

We would like to thank the Kauffman Foundation and the University of California, Berkeley, for financial support.